Better H Gardens*®

A Grower's Guide to Flowering Shrubs

Text by Margaret Hanks
Photographs by Lorna Rose

MURDOCH BOOKS®
Sydney • London • Vancouver • New York

CONTENTS

KEY TO LIFE CYCLE TABLES

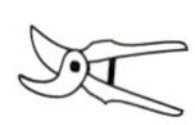

PRUNING

FLOWERING

Life cycle charts are your quick guide.
For full information, consult the accompanying text.

GUIDE TO PLANT SHAPES

These diagrams are used on each page to give a quick guide to the shape of the mature plant.

LEFT: A brilliant clash of spring colour comes from this thoughtful planting of azaleas and standard trailing lantana, with pieris in the background.

GROWING FLOWERING SHRUBS

A lovely garden can be created almost entirely of shrubs. Shrubs give the garden form and definition, and flowering shrubs contribute its essential character. Plan carefully, and you can have some shrubs in flower every month of the year, even if the winter garden lacks the colour and abundance of the spring one.

Shrubs are usually defined as perennial woody plants. They are frequently multi-stemmed, but not always, and the line between tall shrubs and small trees is rather vague—gardeners and professional horticulturists do not always agree. Shrubs may be evergreen or deciduous; their leaves may be small or large, glossy or dull, and they come in an enormous range of shapes. Some shrubs, such as hibiscus, have large showy flowers, while others, such as box, have tiny insignificant ones. Some are grown for their aromatic foliage and some for their heavily scented flowers.

Shrubs come in every shape and size and there is a shrub to suit every situation. When you are planning your garden, select shrubs to suit the particular position. Will the shrub thrive in full sun or does it prefer shade? Consider how high and wide it will grow. Shrubs can take up to 5–10 years to mature, by which we mean that the shrub looks well established and has assumed its final shape, and so whatever you do, don't buy a large-growing shrub for a small space thinking you will keep it pruned. You will get tired of pruning and end up removing it.

LEFT: Shrubs provide an elegant structure for this garden while annuals add splashes of colour.

ABOVE: Brilliant red 'Marina Prior' roses.

PROPAGATION

Most garden shrubs are grown from cuttings. They may be grown from soft-tip cuttings (e.g. hydrangea, fuchsia), semi-hardwood cuttings (the vast majority) or from dormant hardwood cuttings (deciduous shrubs). In some cases the time for taking the cuttings is critical.

Cuttings should be taken from strong, healthy plants, preferably from stems that have not flowered. Soft-tip and semi-hardwood cuttings should be from 5 to 10 cm long, while hardwood cuttings of dormant wood may be up to half a metre long in plants such as japonica but are usually 20–30 cm long. Take cuttings early in the morning. If you are not able to pot them up at once, wrap them in damp newspaper and keep them in a cool place.

Remove all but the topmost leaves and if the leaves are large, as in hydrangeas, you may need to cut these top leaves in half. On the base of the cutting make a sharp, clean, slanting cut just below a node on the stem. Prepare a mix of three parts of coarse washed sand or perlite and one part of peatmoss or peat substitute. Place the mix in a pot, make holes with a pencil where cuttings are to go, insert cuttings to about one-third of their length and then firm the mix around the stem. You can place several cuttings in the one pot. Water the cuttings, drain and set the pot in a warm, sheltered, light place out of direct sun. Keep moist but not wet.

In warm weather roots may form within two to four weeks on some soft-tip cuttings. Hardwood cuttings taken in winter to early spring may take many weeks or months to make roots. Leaves may form long before any roots develop. Don't be tempted to move or plant out these cuttings until you know that they are well rooted. This will be evident either by continued strong leaf and stem development or by roots protruding through drainage holes of the pot.

Some roses will grow quite readily from cuttings but others will not grow vigorously on their own roots. Commercial nurseries 'bud' roses onto rootstocks of wild or species roses. (Budding is a form of grafting using dormant leaf buds.)

Some shrubs may be grown from seed, but this method is only practical with straight species of shrubs as seedlings of the cultivars (cultivated varieties) rarely come true to type.

CHOOSING A PLANT

When choosing a plant at a nursery, the biggest is not always the best. Look for plants that are well shaped and have a good cover of healthy leaves. Avoid plants that have woody roots protruding from the drainage holes, those that are excessively tall for the pot size and those that have knobbly, thickened bases to their stems. All these features show that the plant is pot bound and that it should have been moved into a larger container some time ago. Grevilleas, banksias and waratahs are good examples of shrubs best planted out when they are small as they resent root disturbance. But all plants suffer from transplanting shock and can be badly set back, even when they receive careful treatment. As a rough guide, choose plants that are in pots no larger than 200 mm in diameter.

Azaleas, camellias, hibiscus and many other shrubs are best selected when they are in bloom to ensure that you are getting the variety you want. However, most roses are sold in winter, bagged or bare-rooted in their dormant state. Visit display gardens during the flowering season to select and note your favourites for purchase the following winter.

SOIL PREPARATION

As most shrubs are fairly long lived and form the permanent framework of the garden, it is worth putting some effort into soil preparation. Few shrubs tolerate heavy, waterlogged soil. If drainage is poor you may need to consider raising the planting area or installing subsoil drains. Heavy clay soils can be improved by the addition of gypsum at the rate of 200–300 g per square metre and by working in large quantities of well-rotted organic material. Organic matter should be dug in well ahead of planting time, perhaps two or three weeks ahead in summer and six weeks or so in winter. Sandy soils with poor water and nutrient retention benefit greatly by the addition of large amounts of organic matter before planting. All plants and soils benefit from mulching. Organic mulches of rotted animal manure, compost, leaves, straw or decayed grass clippings give plants the most benefit.

TYPES OF CUTTINGS

CUTTINGS. 1. Nodal cuttings are made by making a sharp cut just below a node or joint. 2. Heel cuttings are pulled from the stem with old wood at the base. 3. Softwood cuttings are cut off from the tip (if the stem bends, the wood is too old).

PLANTING

With good soil preparation and correct planting techniques your shrubs should flourish. Container-grown shrubs can be planted out into the garden at almost any time of the year, except in areas that experience very heavy frost in winter. In these frost-prone areas it is best to avoid planting out anything other than dormant deciduous plants during winter.

- Check that the position you have chosen for your shrub suits its requirements in terms of sun or shade, shelter, drainage and area available for growth.
- Dig a hole at least twice as wide as the potted plant and about the same depth. Loosen soil in the bottom of the hole but don't dig down into a clay layer or you may create a well in which the plant roots will drown.
- Do not put compost or manure in the hole; blood and bone or slow release fertiliser may be sprinkled in the bottom of the hole but it must be covered by 3–5 cm of soil so that the roots do not come into direct contact with the fertiliser.
- Thoroughly water the plant in its pot, loosen the soil by tapping the base and sides of the pot, and then slide the plant out gently. Carefully tease out the roots, cutting vertically down the side of the rootball if necessary; remove thick matted roots from the base.
- Place the plant in the hole so that the soil level is the same as it was in the container. Backfill the hole with soil you have dug out and firm soil in well, but don't crush the roots by stamping around.
- Water thoroughly again to eliminate air pockets and settle the soil.
- Mulch the area around the shrub but keep the mulch well clear of the stem. Organic mulches such as manures and composts give the most benefit to the soil and, therefore, the plant. They break down in time and need replacing at least once a year.

STRIKING A CUTTING

1. TO TAKE A CUTTING, cut just below a leaf (node or joint). Be sure the stem is not bruised, and trim the end of the cutting with a razor blade if need be.

2. INSERT THE CUTTING into a pot, first making a hole with your finger and then firming the earth gently around the cutting. If placing more than one cutting in the pot, space them around the edge.

3. WATER THE CUTTINGS in well but gently, taking care not to dislodge them. Make sure the container has adequate drainage holes so that the excess water will drain away. If the soil remains too wet, the cuttings will rot.

4. MAKE A WIRE OR BAMBOO FRAME that fits around the container and is tall enough to clear the cuttings. Place a polythene bag over the frame and container: the bag will keep the air and soil moist so that it does not dry out. Place pot out of direct sun.

A LATE SPRING BORDER in blue and gold is dominated by the pride of Madeira (Echium fastuosum)*, with yellow alyssum at its feet. Lavender and blue ajuga add further touches of blue to this lovely coolish climate garden.*

MAINTENANCE

Newly planted shrubs should be kept moist but not soggy. They may need daily watering for the first 10–14 days, depending on the weather. Gradually decrease the frequency of watering as they become established until they are receiving a heavy soaking only once a week. After the first couple of summers they may be able to go for two or three weeks without watering, depending on the variety, soil and weather conditions. However, in very hot weather shrubs such as azaleas or fuchsias may need watering more often than once a week. With observation you will become accustomed to the needs of your shrubs.

Wait four or six weeks after planting before you apply fertiliser. Complete plant foods, blood and bone or pelletted poultry manure are suitable for most shrubs, but avoid using poultry manure for acid-loving plants such as azaleas, camellias, gardenias and daphnes. Grevilleas, hakeas, banksias and waratahs are very sensitive to fertilisers and to phosphorus in particular. Mulch them with decayed leaf mould; if you need to fertilise, choose a fertiliser low in phosphorus.

PRUNING

Pruning is not done as a matter of course and many shrubs will never need pruning at all unless it is needed to rejuvenate very old plants or to remove the odd wayward stem. However, if you want or need to prune you cannot go wrong if you prune your shrubs immediately after flowering. The only exception to this is plants such as firethorn and cotoneaster that are grown for their berries, which form after the flowers have faded. They rarely need pruning, and shaping can be done at almost any time.

To train shrubs to a single stem or create a standard you must select a young plant that has a straight stem with as little lateral branching as possible. Then carefully cut or rub off all the lateral growth on the stem, leaving only the top growth intact. You may need to tie the stem to a light stake inserted carefully beside the stem. As the plant grows, keep rubbing or cutting off shoots below the leading growth until the stem is the height you want. Then concentrate on pinching out tips of the top growth as it develops, to gradually create a rounded shape.

KEY TO LIFE CYCLE TABLES

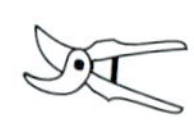

PRUNING

FLOWERING

Life cycle charts are your quick guide.
For full information, consult the accompanying text.

WHAT CAN GO WRONG?

Yellow leaves

- Plants may have been overwatered or they may be too dry.
- Plants may need feeding; fertilise the plant if this has not been done for two or three months and see if there is any improvement within the next two or three weeks.
- Older leaves on shrubs such as gardenias may turn bright yellow before dropping off. Don't worry, they have finished their useful life.
- When the new leaves on azaleas or gardenias are pale yellow but the veins are green, they probably need a dose of iron chelates used according to the directions on the label.

Curled or distorted leaves

- Look for aphids, small sticky insects clustering on the new growth. Wash them off with a hose, spray them with soapy water or use an insecticidal soap or pyrethrum spray.
- Some virus diseases manifest themselves this way and there is no cure for viruses in plants. Consult reference books or a nursery to see whether your plant is likely to have this problem.
- Check that there has been no drift of any herbicide from nearby spraying. Even very small amounts of spray drift can cause distortions to appear on very sensitive plants such as roses.

Black spots on leaves

- These may be fungal leaf spots. On roses they are probably black spot, a common fungal disease that requires the plants to be sprayed with triforine. If possible, improve air circulation around the plants, avoid wetting the leaves when hosing and avoid watering late in the day. Large brown/black spots on camellia leaves are probably the result of sunburn.

Grey/white powder on leaf surfaces

- This deposit is probably powdery mildew, which affects a wide range of plants. Roses, azaleas, hydrangeas and many other shrubs are prone to this fungal disease. Avoid watering late in the day and spray plants with triadimefon if necessary. Triforine will also control this problem. In humid districts this disease can be a perennial problem.

Mottled leaves

- This is usually associated with sap-sucking insects such as scales, thrips, lace bugs and mites (not true insects). Plants under stress are more frequently attacked by these insects, although lace bug is an almost universal problem on azaleas in most seasons. Stress may be induced in plants by drought or over-watering, or by simply having a plant growing outside its preferred climate or aspect.
- Scales may be flat or rounded in various sizes and colours. Small infestations may be wiped off with a damp cloth. Control severe infestations by spraying plants with white oil or a mixture of white oil and maldison.
- Thrips and lace bugs may be reduced in numbers by hosing up under the leaves of the plant. Suitable sprays for their control include insecticidal soaps, pyrethrins and cyfluthrin.
- Mites can be a particular problem in hot, dry weather and on shrubs that are growing under shelter on verandahs or under the eaves of houses. Hosing the foliage helps to reduce the numbers and may avoid the need for spraying. Sprays containing sulphur can be used if the temperature is not above 28°C. Other suitable sprays include insecticidal soaps and fluvalinate.

Holes in leaves or on leaf margins

- This may be snail or slug damage. Search for snails as they are often quite high up in the foliage of shrubs and so do not take baits. Pick them off by hand. Baits can be used around the base of plants if you do not have a dog.
- Caterpillars, crickets and grasshoppers also chew leaves. You may need to dust your plants on several consecutive nights with derris dust, or spray the plants with carbaryl if damage persists.

Stems and leaves webbed or matted together

- Webbing caterpillars can be a problem with plants such as bottlebrush, paperbark and tea-tree. Sprays are all but useless for this problem. Pull out the webbing with a gloved hand or cut out the whole damaged section. Inspect shrubs several times a year to control this pest in its early stages.

Sooty mould (a dry, black coating on leaf surfaces)

- This grows and feeds on sticky honeydew secreted by sap-sucking insects such as aphids and scales. Once the insect pest is controlled, the sooty mould will gradually weather off. Hosing helps; large-leafed plants can be wiped with a damp cloth.

Sudden death of plant

- If the leaves have turned brown but remain attached to the plant, the plant has probably died of root rot. Plant root systems may have been damaged by excessive watering, from rain or irrigation, quite some time before the plant dies, especially in the cooler months of the year. When stress such as an extremely hot or windy day is experienced, the damaged root system cannot cope and the plant appears to have died almost overnight.
- If a plant is suffering from drought the leaves may be brown and rapidly drop off when the plant is given a good watering. These plants may recover if they have not been water-stressed for too long.

POMEGRANATE FRUITS glow red against the green leaves.

ABELIA

Abelia x grandiflora

THE PRETTY PINK FLOWERS of abelias fall at the end of summer and leave behind reddish calyces for prolonged colour.

QUICK-GROWING ABELIAS with their elegant, glossy foliage and pale bell-shaped flowers are ideal for hedges.

FEATURES

Useful for informal hedges, background planting or in mixed shrub borders, this evergreen shrub with long, arching canes will reach its final size of about 2 m high and wide within 2–3 years. Pale pink flowers are followed by persistent reddish calyces, which give the shrub colour over a long period. The shrub is long lived if old canes are cut out every few years.

CONDITIONS

Climate Not fussy unless exposed to salty winds.

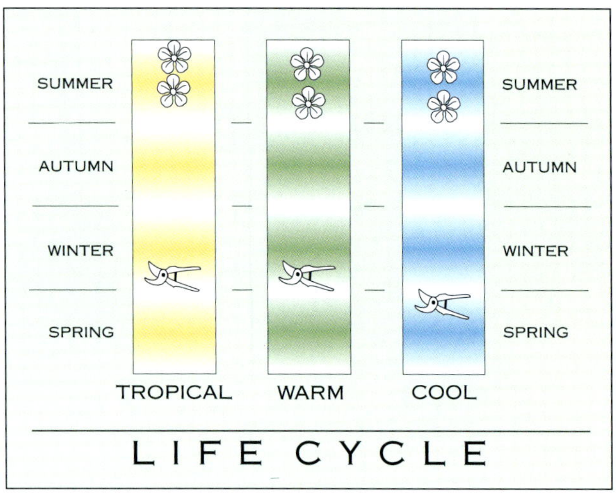

Aspect Prefers full sun and requires at least six hours sun a day to perform well.

Soil Tolerates a wide range of soils but not heavy, wet soil.

GROWING METHOD

Propagation Grow from semi-hardwood cuttings taken from early summer until the middle of autumn. Hardwood cuttings of longer, leafless sections of the canes may be taken in winter.

Watering Once established, tolerates quite dry conditions. Well-established plants require supplementary water only every three or four weeks unless conditions are severe.

Fertilising Use blood and bone or complete plant food in spring, especially during the early years. Once established, abelia tolerates quite poor conditions but responds to feeding.

Problems A very hardy shrub with no special problems.

FLOWERING

Season Long flowering period during summer. The reddish calyx of the flower persists well into early winter.

PRUNING

General In late winter or early spring cut back canes as desired but do not spoil the arching effect. As the plants age it is a good idea to prune out some of the woody old growth at soil level to make way for new growth of young canes.

ARDISIA

Ardisia crenata

USE ARDISIA TO ADD a splash of brilliant red to a shady corner. The tropical shrub is also popular indoors.

GLOSSY, SCARLET BERRIES that stay on the plant all through winter are the star attraction of the compact ardisia.

FEATURES

This evergreen shrub is grown for its attractive foliage and the long-lasting display of bright red berries. It is a small shrub, growing to less than 1 m in height, and as such it is suitable for growing in containers. A long-lived shrub that reaches maturity in 3–5 years, ardisia is a useful feature of shadier gardens, adding colour as well as foliage interest. The flowers and, therefore, the berries usually appear from the first year.

CONDITIONS

Climate Suits milder areas only as it tolerates only the lightest frost.

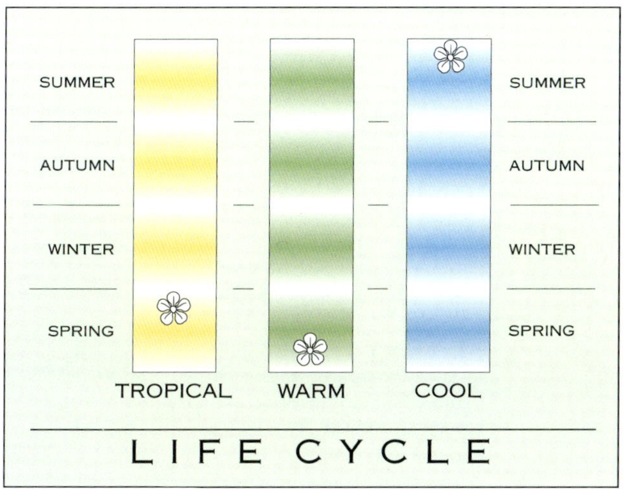

Aspect Prefers a shaded to semi-shaded position sheltered from strong wind. Leaves will burn if exposed to full sun.

Soil Tolerates any reasonably well-drained soil but thrives if the soil is enriched with compost or manure and the plant is mulched.

GROWING METHOD

Propagation Grow from seed sown in spring. Remove the fleshy coverings from the berries and sow the cleaned seed at once.

Watering Needs regular deep watering during summer. A good weekly soak should be sufficient during these hotter months.

Fertilising Apply blood and bone or pelletted poultry manure in late winter to early spring to maintain good healthy growth.

Problems Occasionally plants are attacked by a white wax scale which is readily controlled by wiping the scales off the leaves or by spraying with white oil. Well-grown plants are seldom troubled by pests.

FLOWERING

Season Flowers are fairly insignificant: small white flowers are produced from spring into summer, depending on climate.

Berries Bright red berries form after flowering. They persist on the plant for several months.

PRUNING

General This is not generally necessary except to snip off any wayward stem.

Azalea

Rhododendron hybrids

KURUME AZALEA 'Kirin' is small in flower but the massed blooms make a glorious display during the months of spring.

DECIDUOUS MOLLIS AZALEAS lose their leaves in winter and then greet spring with a mass of brilliantly coloured flowers.

FEATURES

Beloved of gardeners for the beauty of their floral display, azaleas come in a very wide colour range and in sizes varying from about 0.5 m to 2.5 m. They are derived from various species of rhododendron and are among the most widely hybridised plants in the world. These long-lived shrubs reach maturity in 3–5 years and flower from the first year. They can be used in mixed shrub borders, the taller varieties making good background plantings for annuals or smaller perennial plants. The semi-doubles and doubles make excellent pot plant subjects. Flowering plants can be brought inside during the flowering period as temporary indoor decoration but they are not suitable for long-term indoor growing. It is best to buy plants in flower so that you can be sure of getting exactly what you want. Azaleas are often planted with camellias, which enjoy the same soil conditions.

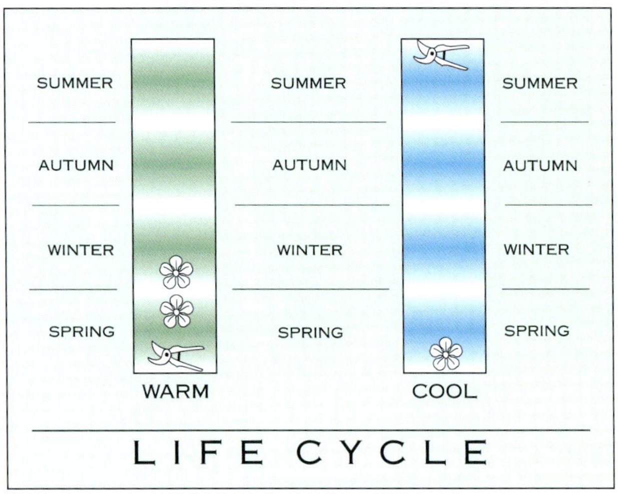

HYBRID GROUPS

Mollis The so-called Mollis azaleas are deciduous and are suitable only for the cooler climates of the world. They grow to about 2 m high and come in bright, clear colours of yellow, orange, red, cream and salmon; many of them flower before the leaves have emerged.

Indica These popular evergreen azaleas flourish in warm to cool areas but are not suitable for the tropics, arid districts or very cold zones. They are available in a dazzling range of colours, in every shade of pink, mauve, purple, crimson, white, salmon and in combinations of colour. Flowers may be single, semi-double or completely double. Some are simple shapes while others are frilled and ruffled.

Kurume The Kurume azaleas have smaller leaves and flowers and a slightly greater cold tolerance than the other evergreen varieties. Flowers are in the same colour range as the Indica azaleas and may be single or 'hose-in-hose', where one flower appears to have been put inside another.

CONDITIONS

Climate Evergreen Indica azaleas are suitable for cool to warm areas, Kurumes tolerate somewhat colder areas and Mollis azaleas are grown successfully only in cool to cold zones.

Aspect The vast majority prefer shelter from strong wind and hot afternoon sun. Semi-shade or dappled sunlight suits them best but there are now 'sun' azaleas that have been specially bred to tolerate sun and more open situations. Of the older varieties, several of the tall, single azaleas, such as 'Magnifica', 'Splendens' and 'Alba Magna', tolerate sun for most of the day if necessary but there can be some flower fading. 'Red Wings' and 'Temperance' are two of the older semi-doubles that tolerate sun.

A RIOT OF SPRING BLOOMS in yellow-orange shades shows why Mollis azaleas are so popular with gardeners.

Soil All azaleas like the same soil conditions. Soil should be well drained but have plenty of well-decayed organic matter added to it before planting. It must be acid soil or plants will not thrive and will suffer from severe iron deficiency. Mulching with a thick layer of organic material, such as rotted animal manure, leaf mould, compost or decayed grass clippings, is essential to keep the roots cool during summer.

GROWING METHOD

Propagation Semi-hardwood cuttings are best taken from early summer to midsummer but they can be taken until early autumn. Propagation by simple layering is also possible if only one or two plants are required.

Watering Must be kept well watered at all times throughout the warmer months without being kept wet. Occasional deep watering is needed in winter too if there is no rain.

Fertilising Use blood and bone or specially formulated azalea and camellia food. Fertilise in early spring as the new growth starts and again in late summer. Do not fertilise later as this may result in a spurt of leaf growth at the expense of the developing flower buds.

Problems Unfortunately azaleas suffer from a number of insect pest and disease problems.
*Azalea petal blight is an ever-present problem in humid areas and is worse in showery weather. This fungal disease causes the flowers to turn to mush and remain stuck on the plant. If you have had petal blight in past seasons and wish to prevent its recurrence you will need to spray the plants with triadimefon (Bayleton®) from the time the buds first show colour and continue spraying according to label directions until flowering has finished.
*Powdery mildew can also be a problem in humid areas but it is usually worse when air flow around plants is poor or the plants are too heavily shaded. Bayleton® will also help to control this problem but improving cultural conditions is the best remedy.
*Fungal leaf gall causes leaves to become swollen, thick and fleshy. The swollen area is pale green with pink overtones. Some varieties are more susceptible than others to this gall and some seasons produce more galls than others. Remove and destroy the galled leaves.
*Azalea lace bug damages the foliage of both azaleas and rhododendrons during spring, summer and into autumn in mild seasons. Leaves are badly mottled in greyish white. Black or brown shiny spots, which are the excreta of the insect, are seen on the underside of the leaf. When damage first appears it may be possible to reduce the number of insects by hosing up under the leaves, otherwise you would need to spray with insecticidal soap, pyrethrins or cyfluthrin.
*Thrips cause damage to the leaves, too. The damage is similar to that of lace bug but the leaves may have a more silvery appearance. Spraying with cyfluthrin should control thrips but in dry, warm weather when they multiply rapidly you may need to repeat the spray.
*Two-spotted mites, commonly known as red spider mites, also suck sap from the leaves. Mites are more prevalent in hot, dry weather and plants growing in sheltered spots, under eaves or under the protection of other plants will be more badly damaged as a rule. If the plants are not in flower when mite attack occurs, hosing up under the leaves every couple of days will help reduce numbers. Insecticidal soap or fluvalinate should give control over this pest. With a magnifying glass it is possible to see the mites on the underside of the leaf. They are like tiny, almost colourless spiders, with two black spots on their backs, and their clear, round eggs can be seen too.

FLOWERING

Season Semi-doubles and doubles may 'spot' flower during autumn and winter with the main flush in spring. Tall single types flower in early spring. Kurumes may 'spot' flower but give their best display in late winter and early spring. Mollis hybrids flower in spring.

PRUNING

General Cutting flowers for the vase is usually as much pruning as is needed, but azaleas can be pruned immediately after flowering if necessary. Old, overgrown shrubs can be rejuvenated by cutting back fairly hard and removing all thin, spindly growth from the centre of the bush. They should not be cut so hard as to leave only woody stems with no leaves. If in doubt, cut half the stems and wait until new growth is forced from the base before cutting the rest. Wayward stems may be cut back at any time of the year. Some gardeners use clippers on the Kurume types as there is so much small, twiggy growth. This is satisfactory and produces rounded bushes.

AZALEA

RIGHT: 'Pink Dream' is a lovely silvery mauve-pink with very large individual flowers. Spot flowering of this fine cultivar may begin in winter before the main flush of blooms.

BELOW: This brilliant azalea cultivar is unusual in that it has a clearly defined white centre. The white makes a startling contrast to the bright main colour.

RIGHT: Only Mollis azaleas come in shades of orange and yellow. This beautiful golden example will add a delightful touch to the garden, mixing well with other colours.

VARIETIES

LEFT: *Few azaleas can surpass the lovely cultivar 'Happy Days' for depth and richness of colour. It can be grown successfully in pots or planted directly in the ground.*

BELOW: *The glorious truss of bright yellow blooms on this Mollis azalea would light up even the dullest garden. These shrubs are one of the delights of spring in a cool climate garden.*

LEFT: *'Ruth Kirk' is one of the older varieties of azalea but it has never gone out of favour. The buds are almost vermilion in colour but they open to the softest shade of pink.*

BANKSIA

Banksia

STRIKING SPIKES of golden banksia flowers give warm colour throughout autumn and winter. Planting these shrubs is an excellent way to attract birds.

BANKSIA in its natural bushland setting. It is also easy to grow in the garden.

FEATURES

The 75 species of banksias range from quite large trees to groundcovers. Time to maturity varies with the species but, if given the right conditions, most will flower after 2–3 years and are long lived. Some of the most spectacular are from dry, rather arid areas and can be difficult to grow in humid districts. *B. ericifolia*, *B. marginata* and *B. spinulosa* are excellent garden shrubs, with leathery leaves and dense spikes of flowers in lovely shades of burnt orange, cream and yellow. Banksias attract birds to the garden.

CONDITIONS

Climate Depends on species. Some need a warm climate; some tolerate cooler conditions and some frost. Many tolerate coastal conditions.

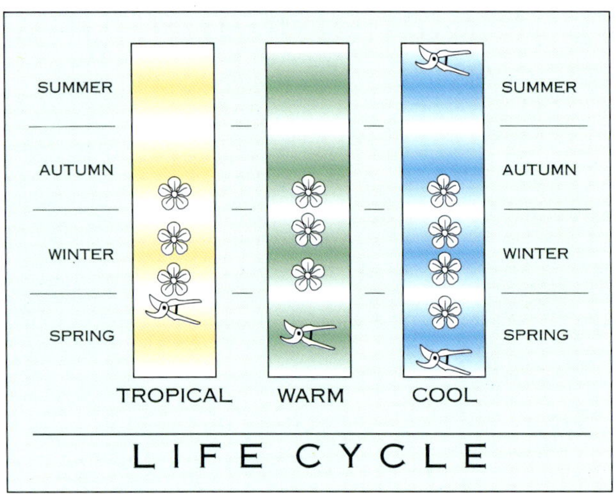

Aspect Prefers full sun but tolerates shade for part of the day.

Soil Must have well-drained soil. Mulch around plants with decayed compost or leaf mould.

GROWING METHOD

Propagation Can be grown from seed. The mature woody cones (follicles) can be placed in paper bags in the sun or in a warm oven so that the seeds will be released. Seeds sown in a fast-draining mix germinate fairly readily. Plant out seedlings into their permanent position once they are large enough to handle to avoid constricting roots.

Watering Water regularly to establish, but once established banksias need only occasional deep waterings to do well.

Fertilising Banksias are sensitive to fertilisers in general and to phosphorus in particular. Don't fertilise at all if they are growing well. If you feel you must fertilise, use only fertilisers that are low in phosphorus.

Problems Banksias are very prone to root rot in poorly drained soils. Leaves may be chewed by various caterpillars but they can usually be controlled by hand picking.

FLOWERING

Season The species mentioned have a long flowering period through autumn and winter.

PRUNING

General Prune to shape after flowering, if necessary, but the natural shape does not generally need alteration. Flowers can be cut for the vase and this is a form of pruning.

BARBERRY

Berberis thunbergii

A SHRUB for all seasons—the small yellow flowers are followed by bright red berries.

BARBERRY BUSHES can be trimmed into a formal hedge but the flowers will be most effective if the plant is allowed, as it is here, to grow freely and naturally.

FEATURES

The most commonly grown of the ornamental barberries, *B. thunbergii* is a dense, rounded, deciduous shrub about 1 m high and wide with sharp spines on the stems. Long lived, it reaches maturity in about 5 years and flowers from early in its life. It has small, bright yellow flowers and the leaves colour well in autumn in cool areas. The form with reddish-purple leaves, known as 'Atropurpurea', is widely grown for foliage contrast. It is ornamental in a mixed planting and its spiky nature makes it useful as a low hedge. The bright red berries persist on the shrub through winter, making it an attractive addition to the garden in every season.

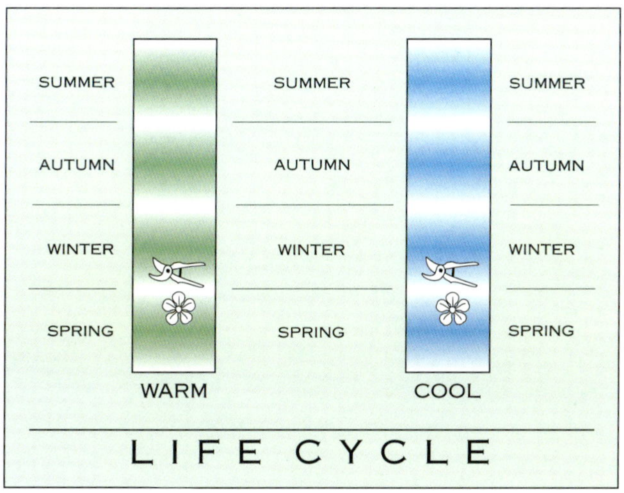

CONDITIONS

Climate Not suitable for the tropics but should grow well in a wide range of other climates. It is very frost tolerant.

Aspect Needs full sun to be shown to best advantage.

Soil Tolerates a wide range of soil conditions but will grow much better in a soil enriched with organic matter.

GROWING METHOD

Propagation The straight green species can be grown from seed if the berries ripen on the bush and the seeds are cleaned and planted when fresh. Hardwood cuttings taken from middle to late winter should strike readily.

Watering Although barberries tolerate drought, regular summer watering produces a much more attractive plant.

Fertilising Apply complete plant food in early spring and again in midsummer for best growth.

Problems Plants can be attacked by scale insects, which can be controlled by spraying with white oil.

FLOWERING

Season The bright yellow flowers are produced during the spring months.

PRUNING

General Many growers clip these shrubs into rounded shapes but they do not have to be pruned. Late winter would be the best time for shearing but tidying up can be done at any time.

Bauhinia

Bauhinia galpinii

SHOW-OFF FLOWERS: the bright salmon red blooms of this bauhinia sit proudly atop the lush green foliage.

A MATURE BAUHINIA is used here to provide truly spectacular but low-maintenance camouflage for a mundane wooden fence.

FEATURES

Many bauhinias are tree-like but *B. galpinii* is an evergreen shrub growing to 2 m or so high and up to 3 m wide. It flowers after 2–3 years and reaches maturity in about 5 years. This long-lived shrub can be grown as a specimen or against a wall where it can spread if given some support. Ideal in tropical gardens, it also grows well in other warm, frost-free areas.

CONDITIONS

Climate Best in very warm areas; dislikes cold areas.

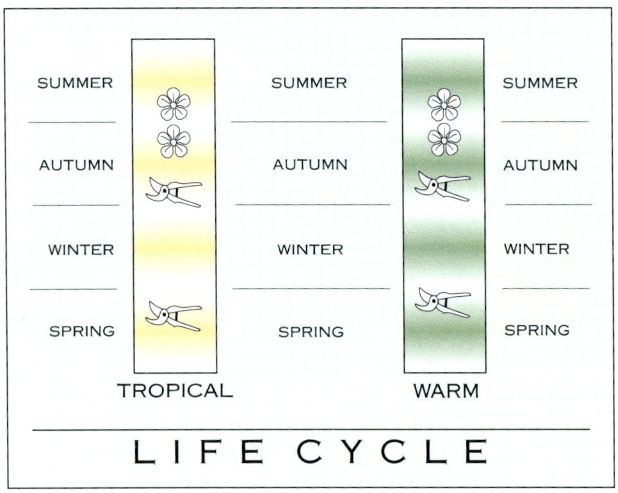

Aspect Needs full sun and warmth. Out of tropical areas it should have protection from the coldest winter winds.

Soil Well-drained soil rich in organic matter gives best results.

GROWING METHOD

Propagation Grow from seed, which needs to ripen in its pod on the shrub. Once pods are dry and brown, remove seed, soak overnight in warm water and sow in a good seed-raising mix.

Watering Give a deep weekly soaking during the warmer months but it tolerates dry periods remarkably well. In winter, especially outside tropical areas, you will need to water perhaps only once a month.

Fertilising Apply complete plant food or blood and bone in early spring and again in midsummer.

Problems No particular pests or diseases.

FLOWERING

Season The bright salmon red flowers are produced from midsummer until early autumn. The flowers sit on top of the foliage giving a striking effect.

PRUNING

General Light pruning may be carried out immediately after flowering finishes. Do any heavier pruning in early spring.

Begonia

Begonia coccinea

WAVY-EDGED, VARIEGATED LEAVES are attractive in their own right—the bright, waxy flowers of the begonia are an added bonus.

SHRUBBY BEGONIAS are retiring plants, which will thrive in shady, protected spots in the garden.

FEATURES

Sometimes misleadingly called tree begonia, this shrub grows to 2–2.5 m high, with straight, cane-like stems. In good conditions it can reach maturity in 2 years and can be constantly rejuvenated by removing old stems. The slightly succulent leaves have wavy edges and the flowers hang in waxy trusses. Begonia grows well in sheltered, somewhat shady gardens. Other shrubby begonias worth growing are *B. fuchsioides*, with small pink and white fuchsia-like flowers for many months of the year, and *B. scharffii*, with reddish, hairy stems and trusses of white and red flowers.

CONDITIONS

Climate Suits warm, humid climates but has little or no frost tolerance.

Aspect Needs protection from strong wind and hot afternoon sun. Does well in dappled sunlight.

Soil Needs well-drained soil and does best in soils with high organic matter content. Heavy clay soils are not suitable for these begonias.

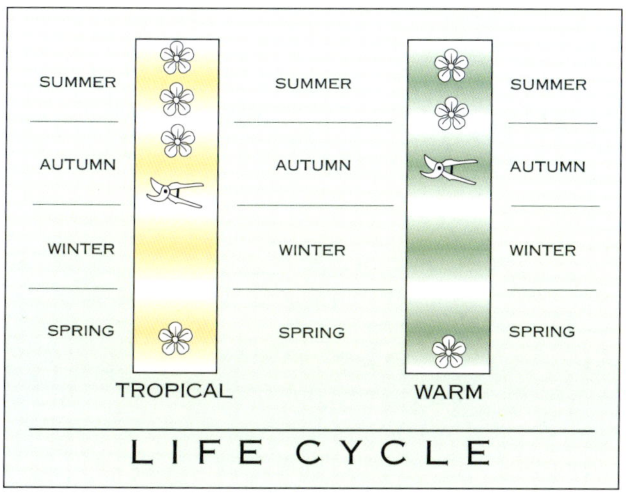

GROWING METHOD

Propagation Most begonias grow fairly easily from tip cuttings taken almost any time of the year except winter. Large clumps can be divided up and sections replanted but you need to cut the canes down to about 10–15 cm in height.

Watering Give a deep watering once a week in summer but only occasionally in winter. They do not tolerate overwatering as their fibrous roots rot.

Fertilising Lightly fertilise with blood and bone in early spring and again in midsummer. A mulch of rotted compost or manure provides nutrients as well as good conditions for the fibrous roots.

Problems Overwatering or poorly drained soil kills these plants. No special pest problems but they are sometimes affected by powdery mildew if air circulation is poor and they are too shaded. Improve conditions and spray with triadimefon (Bayleton®) if necessary.

FLOWERING

Season Long flowering period from middle of spring right through until late autumn in good conditions. The species has bright red flowers but there are a number of varieties with flowers in white, pink, deep rose and orange.

PRUNING

General Remove spent flowers at any time. Older plants with 'leggy' canes can be rejuvenated by cutting out some of the older canes at ground level. Canes can also be shortened by cutting them just above a node on the stem, after flowering in autumn or in early spring.

Bird of Paradise

Strelitzia reginae

THE GLAMOROUS bird of paradise flower looks uncannily like a haughty, long-necked bird that has fluttered in to grace the garden with its elegant presence.

STRELITZIA PARVIFOLIA has smaller leaves, the better to show off its flowers.

FEATURES

Bird of paradise has spectacular bright orange and blue flowers, which have a bird-like shape. Long lived, it may take several years to mature and flower. The bluish green, paddle-like leaves are also distinctive, creating a strong textural effect. The shrub grows to only just over 1 m high but it can form a clump 2 m or more wide. It can be grown as a lawn specimen in large gardens or against a wall.

CONDITIONS

Climate Not suitable for cold zones. It performs best in warm areas, including the tropics.

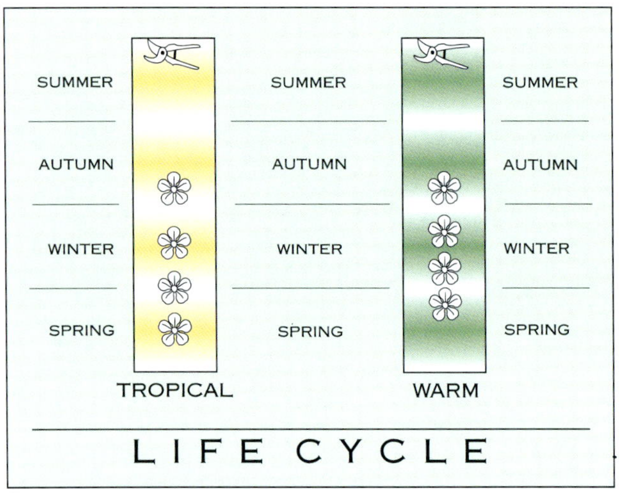

Aspect To get the best results it must be in full sun all day and it should be sheltered from very cold winds.

Soil Tolerates a range of soils but not heavy clays. It does best in well-drained soil that has been enriched with organic matter.

GROWING METHOD

Propagation Can be grown from seed but is usually grown from divisions of older clumps. Lift clumps in late winter and divide into sections—each section must have roots attached. Cut down the stems and give the new divisions lots of care until they are established.

Watering Give heavy weekly watering during the warmer months but only occasional watering during winter.

Fertilising Any form of complete plant food is suitable; apply in early spring and again in midsummer.

Problems No particular pest or disease problems.

FLOWERING

Season The unusual orange and blue flowers appear from autumn until late in the following spring. Flowers are long lasting and are very popular for use in large-scale and formal floral arrangements.

PRUNING

General Spent flower stems or untidy leaves should be cut out at ground level in early summer, otherwise no pruning is necessary.

Blue Butterfly Bush

Clerodendrum ugandense

SPRAYS OF FLOWERS in two shades of clear blue attract butterflies, giving this bush its common name.

BLUE BUTTERFLY BUSH rewards gardeners with a long flowering season from late spring to early autumn. This east African shrub needs pruning to keep its compact shape.

FEATURES

The two-toned blue flowers with their long stamens are a very attractive feature of the blue butterfly bush, and the long flowering period throughout summer makes this a refreshing addition to warm climate gardens. Moreover, this shrub flowers when still young, thus increasing its garden value. Branched like a small tree, it reaches maturity in about 2 years and grows 2–3 m high. It has a medium life span. Blue butterfly bush is evergreen and looks most effective when grown on its own or in mixed plantings.

CONDITIONS

Climate Best in tropical to warm areas. Quite unsuitable for cool zones.

Aspect Needs shelter from strong, cold wind and is at its best in full sun.

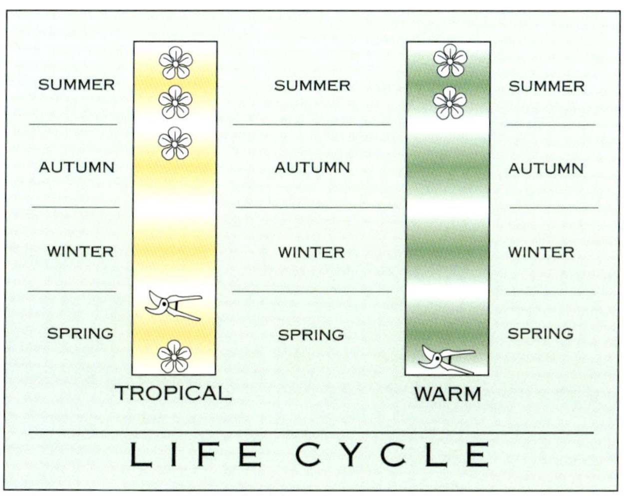

Soil Needs well-drained soil, preferably with a high organic content. Mulching with manure or compost helps to provide the conditions it prefers best.

GROWING METHOD

Propagation Easily grown from seed (it sometimes self-sows) or from semi-hardwood cuttings that are taken during the late summer and early autumn months.

Watering Needs regular deep watering in summer about once a week. It should be watered occasionally in dry winters but should never be too wet, especially in cold weather.

Fertilising Apply blood and bone, pelletted poultry manure or complete plant food in early spring and again in midsummer.

Problems No particular pests or diseases.

FLOWERING

Season Long flowering period from late spring until early autumn.

PRUNING

General Do not prune before the weather has warmed up in spring as these plants are sensitive to cold. They can be pruned to shape any time during the warm months and indeed they usually need reducing by about one-third to keep a compact bushy shape.

HINT

Blue flowers Blue flowered shrubs tend to stand out in a summer garden. This one is a great foil for plants with dark foliage or hot flower colours, such as hibiscus or other tropical plants.

Boronia

Boronia

MODEST BROWN BORONIA FLOWERS give off a delicious, permeating perfume.

NOT ALL BORONIAS are brown: here Boronia ledifolia, *the Sydney boronia, shows off its mass of lovely, star-shaped and jewel coloured flowers. They have a spicy perfume.*

FEATURES

Many species of boronia are grown for their scented flowers and/or foliage. They flower early and can reach maturity within 2 years. They can, however, be short lived and the fragrant brown boronia (*B. megastigma*) from Western Australia can be very difficult to grow in many areas, particularly in humid coastal regions. Boronias can be grown in the garden or in containers, where it may be easier to provide conditions that suit their somewhat exacting requirements. Look in local nurseries to find a suitable boronia.

CONDITIONS

Climate Depends on species; none suits tropical areas.

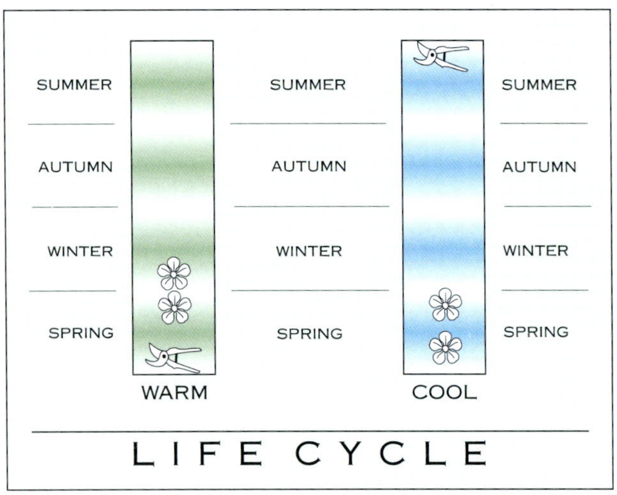

Aspect They need morning sun and afternoon shade, or dappled sunlight for most of the day. Shelter from strong wind is an essential growing requirement for all of these shrubs.

Soil Soil must be very well drained but should retain some moisture at all times. This is the requirement that is hardest to meet. Mulching around plants with stones or pebbles can be useful as organic mulches tend to cause rots around stems.

GROWING METHOD

Propagation Can be grown from tip cuttings taken from late spring into midsummer.

Watering Require regular water during the warmer months but do not tolerate overwatering. Keep them drier in winter but do not allow soil to become powder-dry.

Fertilising A very light dusting of blood and bone may be applied in late spring after flowering, but it is not essential.

Problems They are prone to root rot but there are no other particular pest or disease problems.

FLOWERING

Season Boronias are spring-flowering shrubs but some will begin flowering in the middle of winter. You can expect that most boronias will flower some time between late winter and the end of spring.

PRUNING

General Prune lightly after flowering but never cut into the heavier stems.

Bottlebrush

Callistemon

BOTTLEBRUSH FLOWERS are most commonly bright red but they can also be burgundy, pink or cream. It is obvious how these evergreen shrubs came by their common name.

THIS HANDSOME SHRUB flourishes if planted in full sun.

FEATURES

While in flower bottlebrushes produce copious amounts of nectar and attract honey-eating birds to the garden. There are many species and a great range of cultivars, with flowers mainly in bright reds but also in shades of pink, cream and burgundy. There is probably a bottlebrush to suit most gardens and some of the small-growing varieties such as 'Little John' can be grown in containers. Heights range from about 60 cm for 'Little John' to about 2 m for 'Captain Cook', but the majority grow to about 3–4 m. These shrubs flower early and mature in about 5 years. They are long lived if conditions are suitable.

CONDITIONS

Climate Depends on species. Many tolerate light frost but need protection during the first winter.

Aspect For best flowering they need full sun all day.

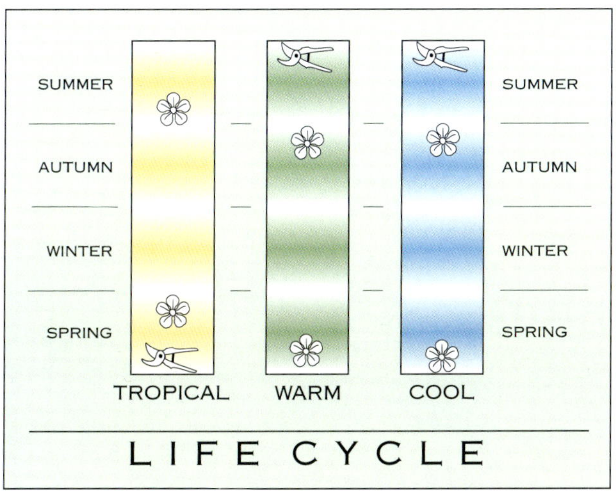

Soil Tolerate a wide range of soils and perform well even in heavier clay, but best in lighter soils.

GROWING METHOD

Propagation The species are easily grown from seed but the named varieties must be grown from cuttings, which are best taken as semi-hardwood cuttings in late summer and early autumn.

Watering Regular watering is needed for establishment. They tolerate long, dry periods but growth and flowering is best if given heavy waterings every couple of weeks in warm months.

Fertilising They cope quite well without added fertiliser but respond to a light application of blood and bone in late winter and at the end of summer.

Problems Webbing caterpillars may damage plants in some seasons. Cut out or pull out the webbed leaves and frass: spraying is not effective. Callistemon sawfly, which generally appears in early autumn, can defoliate plants if they are not detected early enough. Try picking off the larvae and destroy them by dropping into a container of water with some kerosene added.

FLOWERING

Season Main flowering flush is middle to late spring but there is often a smaller flush of flowers during autumn.

PRUNING

General If you wish to prune, do so as soon as the flowers fade because new growth appears from the top of the flower. Some cutting back does help to keep the growth greener and more compact. Cut thin, spindly, dead wood out of the centre of the plant. Old shrubs can be cut back quite hard to rejuvenate them, but don't remove all the leaf growth at the same time.

Box

Buxus sempervirens; B. microphylla var. *japonica*

THE DARK, POINTY LEAVES of English box are its main growing feature. They dominate the tiny flowers.

CREATIVE CLIPPING has here established strongly defined lines and transformed these box plants into a traditional, formal topiary hedge.

FEATURES

Both English box (*B. sempervirens*) and Japanese box (*B. microphylla* var. *japonica*) can grow very tall but are usually seen as clipped hedges or as topiary. They are very long lived but slow growing, reaching 1 m or so within 5 years. Both have small leaves: English box has darker, more pointed leaves and Japanese box shiny, lighter green, more rounded leaves. The flowers are small, lightly perfumed and very attractive to bees. Box plants are often grown in containers.

CONDITIONS

Climate English box prefers cool to cold areas; Japanese box, although cold tolerant, prefers mild areas. Not suitable for very warm areas.

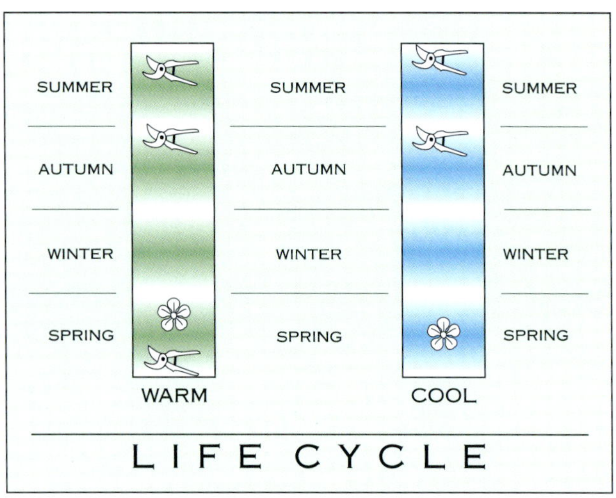

Aspect Needs full sun to maintain its compact growth habit.

Soil Tolerates a wide range of soil conditions but does best in well-drained soil with some organic content.

GROWING METHOD

Propagation Can be grown from seed but is best grown from semi-hardwood cuttings that are taken at any time during the months of late spring or autumn.

Watering Established plants tolerate fairly dry conditions but they are best if given regular deep watering during the warmer months. Container-grown plants must be kept well watered, especially during the warmer summer months.

Fertilising Blood and bone or complete plant food may be applied in early spring and again in midsummer. These plants are, however, not heavy feeders and they will get along quite well, even if you should forget to fertilise them at all.

Problems No particular problems.

FLOWERING

Season Flowering time is spring but the flowers are very insignificant in appearance.

PRUNING

General Can be clipped at any time to maintain a formal shape. If you are growing box as a hedge or in any clipped shape, use hedge clippers instead of trying to cut each stem with secateurs.

BUTTERFLY BUSH

Buddleja davidii

THE LIGHT PURPLE FLOWERS of the butterfly bush or mock lilac smell of honey and are irresistible to butterflies.

WHILE THE FLOWERS are the reason the butterfly bush is popular, the green leaves with their grey underside are also attractive.

FEATURES

The dull green leaves of this very hardy bush are whitish grey on the underside and they can add foliage interest in a mixed shrub border. The flowers in the species are light purple but many named cultivars are available with flowers in white, rose, purple, dark blue or magenta. The flowers have a somewhat unpleasant smell but are very attractive to butterflies. The bush grows to about 3 m and is often grown with multiple stems. It flowers early in its life, reaching maturity in about 3–5 years. Butterfly bush can be long lived if old canes are cut out regularly.

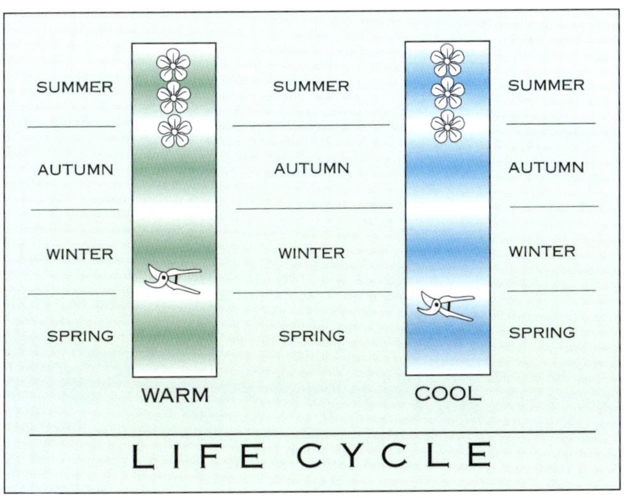

CONDITIONS

Climate Not suitable for tropical gardens but the bush can be grown successfully in both warm and cool districts.

Aspect Performs best when in full sun.

Soil Tolerates most soils but is at its best in a well-drained soil enriched with organic matter. Mulching helps to retain soil moisture during summer months.

GROWING METHOD

Propagation Grows easily from semi-hardwood cuttings taken in autumn or from hardwood cuttings taken in winter.

Watering Regular deep watering during spring and summer should ensure good blooming but it does tolerate dry periods, especially if the soil has been well mulched.

Fertilising Give complete plant food in early spring.

Problems No particular pest or disease problems.

FLOWERING

Season The flowering spikes appear from early summer until the middle of autumn.

PRUNING

General The long canes can be shortened in late winter and any thin, weak growth cut out. You may also cut back immediately after flowering if you prefer.

Californian Lilac

Ceanothus

FLOWERS ARE ALWAYS BLUE, ranging in tone from pale powder blue to a rich deep indigo.

THE BREATH-TAKING BEAUTY of the Californian lilac in full spring bloom—it's a useful plant for inland areas as it thrives under dry conditions.

FEATURES

There are many forms of Californian lilac, from prostrate groundcovers to shrubs 4–5 m tall. All have blue flowers but the colour varies from pale powder blue to deep violet blue. In the right climate they can be long lived, but otherwise they have short lives. They particularly dislike humid, showery summers. These shrubs flower early, but the time to maturity varies with the species.

CONDITIONS

Climate Best in cool to mild climates. Not suitable for the tropics or humid coastal zones.

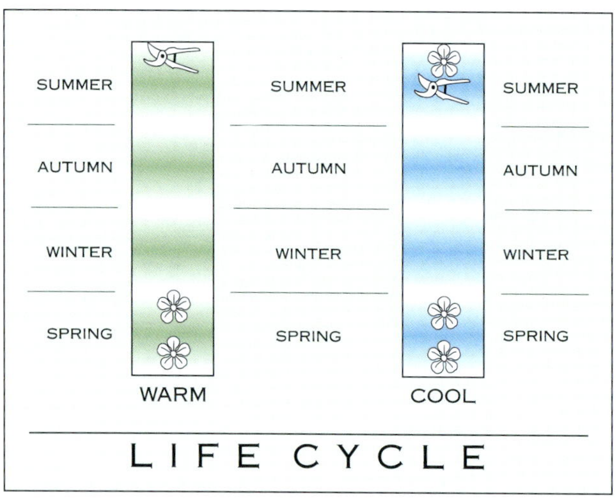

Aspect Must have full sun and they need plenty of good air circulation.

Soil Must have well-drained soil. These plants grow in sandy or gravelly soils but they do not tolerate heavy clay soils that will induce root rot in them.

GROWING METHOD

Propagation The species can be grown from seed but most varieties are grown from semi-hardwood cuttings taken from early summer until the middle of autumn.

Watering In their native habitat these plants receive rain only in winter and are accustomed to very dry summers. In cultivation they should probably be watered every two or three weeks in winter if it is dry and perhaps once a month during the summer months.

Fertilising Apply blood and bone or pelletted poultry manure in late winter.

Problems Very susceptible to root rot but there are no other specific pest or disease problems.

FLOWERING

Season Most varieties flower during middle to late spring but some continue flowering into the summer months.

PRUNING

General Tip prune after the flowers have faded but unruly shoots can be cut off at any time throughout the year.

CAMELLIA

Camellia

THE EXQUISITE BEAUTY of two delicately tinted camellia blossoms: they have fallen onto a bed of clubmoss.

CAMELLIAS AND AZALEAS like living together. Here the aptly named camellia 'Happy' gets along famously with azalea 'Red Wings'.

FEATURES

Camellias are among the most loved and popular shrubs of all. Their glossy green foliage and showy flowers are a great asset in the garden, particularly as the various species can bloom from autumn through to spring. Flowers may be white, pink, deep rose or deep red with many combinations of these colours. These evergreen shrubs range in size from 1 m to 5 or 6 m high, depending on variety; in their habitats some grow into trees 8–10 m tall. Most flower after 2 or 3 years and they reach maturity after 10–20 years. They are very long lived. They make ideal garden plants and can be used as hedges, espaliers, lawn specimens or in pots or mixed shrub borders.

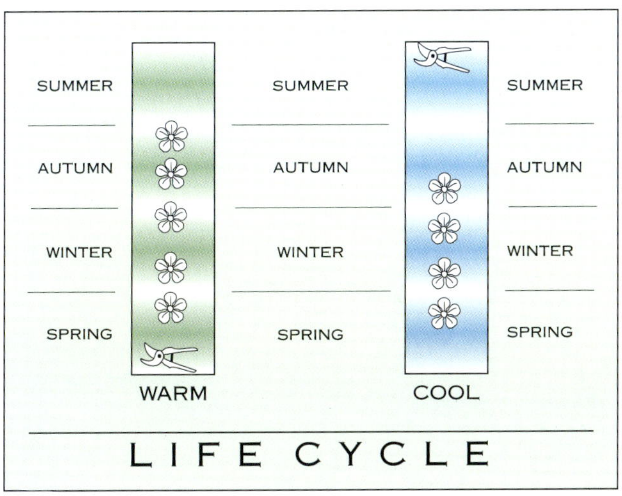

Selection The original camellias came from various parts of China and Japan but they have been widely hybridised to produce an enormous number of cultivars. It is best to select the camellia you want while it is in flower to ensure that you are getting what you want. Specialist camellia nurseries and other large nurseries display flowers during the main flowering season. Choose a variety suited to the position you have in mind and you will have a lovely plant to cherish over many years.

Types There are four main types of camellia: *C. sasanqua*, *C. japonica*, *C. reticulata* and *C.* x *williamsii*. They are each discussed in more detail on pages 28–29.

CONDITIONS

Climate Camellias do extremely well in cool to mild areas with only light frosts. They are not suitable for the tropics, hot, dry areas with low humidity, or the coldest zones, as they prefer a moderate climate.

Aspect They need protection from hot, dry wind and frost. Most grow well in filtered sun although some varieties take full sun. Sasanquas tolerate more sun than most other camellias and reticulatas need full sun for part of the day. Some cultivars of *C. japonica*, such as 'The Czar', 'Great Eastern', 'Moshio' and 'Emperor of Russia', take full sun.

Soil They need slightly acid, well-drained, well-aerated soil that is rich in decayed organic matter. Heavy, badly drained soils cause root rot and often the death of plants.

('Camellia' continues on page 30.)

CAMELLIA

RIGHT: 'Wilamina' is a small formal double cultivar of C. japonica *with incurved petals. Flowers cut well and also hold well on the plant.*

ABOVE: C. japonica *'Nuccio's Gem' is a large white formal double which shows the perfect petal formation of the formal double type. It must be grown in shade and shelter.*

BELOW: 'Scentuous' is a small informal double hybrid of C. japonica *'Tiffany' and the species* C. lutchuensis. *The creamy white flowers have pale pink outer petals and the perfume of* C. lutchuensis. *This is a very profuse bloomer.*

RIGHT: 'Wynne Rayner' is a semi-double hybrid of C. japonica *and* C. sasanqua. *It is classed separately from the reticulata group, although many of them are bred from this cross.*

LEFT: 'Buttons 'n' bows' is a medium-sized formal double hybrid of C. saluenensis. *The deep pink outer petals shade into a creamy white centre. It has a long flowering period.*

Camellia sasanqua

Sasanquas start the season by producing flowers from autumn until the middle of winter, depending on variety. The flowers are fragile and shatter easily but they make a wonderful show in the garden. Flowers may be single, semi-double or double in white, palest pink, rose pink, cerise or scarlet. They are tolerant of a wider range of conditions than the other types. Most of them grow in sun or shade although they do not grow successfully in full sun in hot, dry districts. Sasanquas come in various sizes and forms, from the low, spreading growth of 'Shishi-Gashira' to tall, vigorous shrubs such as 'Plantation Pink' and 'Jennifer Susan', which grow to 5 m or more. The smaller, more compact types make good container plants, they are excellent hedging plants and some cultivars with pendulous growth can be trained as espaliers.

Camellia reticulata

C. reticulata has the largest, most spectacular blooms of all the camellias but the shrubs themselves are more sparse and open in foliage. Many of the more recently developed hybrids are crosses between *C. japonica* and *C. reticulata*, which gives the shrubs denser leaf cover and longer flowering, coupled with very large, showy flowers. Generally *C. reticulata* needs lighter soils with better drainage than the other camellias. These plants make excellent specimen plants and are also ideal for container growing. They also need more direct sun than other camellias.

VARIETIES

BELOW: The formal double C. japonica *'Betty Ridley' is shown here with the tiny pink flower of the species* C. rosiflora *to give an idea of their relative sizes. 'Betty Ridley' is a profusely blooming hybrid* C. japonica *x* sasanqua-reticulata.

ABOVE: 'Star above star' is a cultivar of C. vernalis *usually listed with* C. sasanqua *because of the similarities of growth and uses. Blooming late in the season, it is an upright grower suitable for small gardens and container growing. Flowers are white flushed pink and semi-double.*

BELOW: 'Desire', a large formal double cultivar of C. japonica, *shows mainly white petals, the outer petals being delicately flushed with cerise pink.*

ABOVE: 'Lois Shinault' is a large-flowered cultivar of C. reticulata *with fluted edges on the semi-double orchid-pink flowers and a showy boss of golden stamens in the centre.*

Camellia japonica

This is the species most people think of when camellias are mentioned. There is a staggering number of varieties to choose from in colours of white through palest to darkest pink to deep reds and combinations of these. They are usually classified by flower type, that is, single, semi-double, formal double, paeony form and anemone form. Some camellias produce 'sports', which are flowers of different colour or form on one branch or shoot of the shrub. Some of these sports have been the source of new varieties. Some of the darker flowered camellias are tolerant of quite sunny conditions but the whites and pale pinks should not be planted where their buds receive early morning sun while they are still wet with dew, as this tends to ruin the blooms by browning the buds. *C. japonica* may be grown as a specimen or in a border as a background planting. Some varieties are suitable for tub culture, too. You can select different varieties to give you flowers from late autumn until spring.

Camellia x williamsii

This is a very fine group of camellias bred by crossing *C. japonica* and *C. saluenensis*. The original crosses were made in Cornwall by J.C. Williams who gave them their name. Flowers cover the same colour range as other camellias but most are semi-double in form. Some of the most popular cultivars are 'Donation', 'Elsie Jury', 'E.G. Waterhouse' and 'Water Lily'.

CAMELLIA

(continued from page 27)

SPECTACULAR RUFFLED BLOOMS of Camellia reticulata *'Tataochung'—they're truly the 'show-offs' of the camellia family.*

SMALL, DELICIOUSLY SCENTED FLOWERS such as these are borne by Camellia lutchuensis *from autumn to spring.*

GROWING METHOD

Propagation Semi-hardwood cuttings taken in early summer seem to be the most successful. They may be slow to root but if soil moisture is maintained without sogginess, and sheltered, humid conditions provided, you should have some success. Some varieties are very hard to grow on their own roots and these are generally grafted onto understocks of *C. sasanqua*.

Watering Regular deep watering is needed in the warmer months to ensure a steady soil moisture level. Established plants that are well mulched probably need a deep soaking once a week but younger plants may need twice weekly watering in warm, dry weather.

Fertilising Blood and bone or azalea and camellia food should be applied in early spring and in late summer. In early spring mulch plants well with rotted cow manure, compost or leaf mould, taking care not to allow mulch to pack up around plant stems.

Problems Camellias have relatively few serious insect pest and disease problems but you may encounter some of the following.

*Bud drop: This can be caused by overwet or overdry soils, root rot or root disturbance. Some very late flowering varieties may have the buds literally pushed off the stem by new spring growth.

*Browning of petals and balling of blooms: This usually occurs when buds or flowers receive early morning sun while still wet with dew. Petals may be scorched and some buds 'ball' and fail to open. Some varieties with clusters of big buds are prone to this. Gently breaking off some of the buds when they first form helps to reduce this last problem.

*Oedema: If plants are overwet and conditions are overcast small brown corky swellings may develop on leaves. Reduce watering and try to improve air circulation.

*Scale insects: These may be found on the upper or lower surface of leaves. Scales are sap suckers and can debilitate the plants. Spraying with white oil controls these pests but spray only in cool or cloudy weather so that the oil does not cause sunburn on leaves.

*Leaf gall: This causes abnormal thickening and discolouration of new growth. It occurs in spring and is caused by a fungus. Pick off and destroy affected leaves.

*Virus: Virus infections may be responsible for variable, bright yellow patterns on leaves or for ringspot. Rings develop on leaves and as the leaf ages it becomes yellowish while the centres of the rings become bright green. There is no cure for virus disease but plants rarely lose much vigour or have their blooming affected. You could pick off the worst looking leaves if they are spoiling the appearance of your plants.

FLOWERING

Season Some type of camellia can be in flower any time from early autumn until the middle of spring. The sasanquas start flowering in early autumn, while the last of the japonicas and reticulatas will still be in bloom during the months of spring.

PRUNING

General Little pruning is needed. Cutting blooms for the vase is usually enough to keep plants compact. However, any thin, spindly, unproductive growth can be cut from the centre of the shrub at almost any time. Old, overgrown camellias can be rejuvenated by quite heavy pruning as long as cuts are made directly above a leaf or leaf bud. If severe pruning is needed it may be better to do it in stages rather than shock the plant by removing all its foliage at once.

Cassia

Cassia and *Senna*

CHEERFUL YELLOW Cassia bicapsularis *flowers provide colour in autumn and produce distinctive bean-like seed pods.*

A SUBSTANTIAL SHRUB, Cassia bicapsularis *is attractive year-round. It grows fast but is short lived.*

FEATURES

Cassias are a very large group of plants with mainly bright yellow flowers, although some of the tropical species have pink flowers. They flower early in life, but the time to maturity and the length of their life varies with the species. *S. artemisioides*, native to the inland of Australia, grows to about 1.5 m and is ideal for hot, dry gardens. It has finely divided silvery leaves and yellow flowers from late winter to early summer. *C. bicapsularis* grows to 3 or 4 m. It produces showy, bright yellow flowers in autumn and large numbers of bean-like pods from which seeds germinate readily (avoid growing it close to bushland). *C. fistula*, the golden shower tree, is suitable for the tropics and very warm areas only. The long chains of clear yellow flowers deck this cassia through summer and into early autumn. Other tree-like cassias also produce a bright floral display.

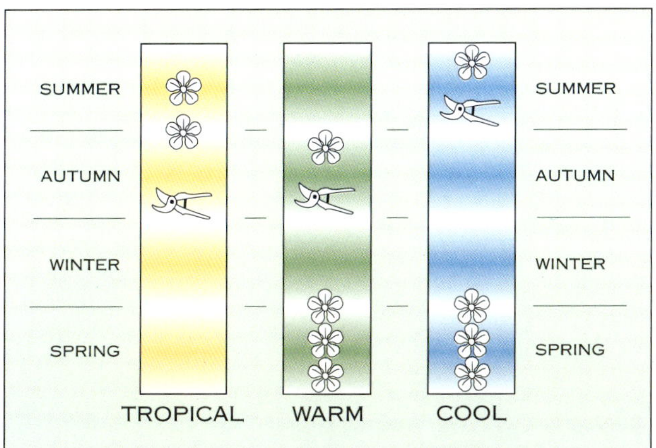

LIFE CYCLE

CONDITIONS

Climate *S. artemisioides* tolerates frost well but other species prefer warm, temperate climates and do not survive very cold weather.

Aspect All cassias do best in full sun all day.

Soil Must have well-drained and well-aerated soil. *C. fistula* performs better if the soil has been well enriched with decayed organic material before planting.

GROWING METHOD

Propagation Cassias grow readily from seed sown in spring. Soak seed at least overnight in warm water to soften the hard seed coat.

Watering *S. artemisioides* tolerates drought extremely well but needs regular watering to establish. *C. fistula* needs ample summer moisture but prefers to be kept on the dry side during winter months.

Fertilising All respond well to additional feeding, preferably in early spring. Any complete plant food may be used. *S. artemisioides* needs only very light feeding.

Problems No particular pest or disease problems.

FLOWERING

Season *S. artemisioides* flowers from late winter until early summer, *C. bicapsularis* in autumn and *C. fistula* throughout the summer months and into early autumn.

PRUNING

General Tip pruning or pruning for shape is all that is necessary for these plants. Prune *C. bicapsularis* immediately after flowering to avoid the formation of seed pods.

Cherry Pie

Heliotropium arborescens

OLD-FASHIONED CHERRY PIE or heliotrope has pretty flowers but it is cherished most for its rich fragrance, which is evocative of vanilla.

IDEAL IN A COTTAGE GARDEN, pretty mauve cherry pie sits delightfully here with sorrel and dill.

FEATURES

Also known as heliotrope, this evergreen, soft-stemmed shrub has fragrant mauve to purple flowers borne over a long season. The fragrance reminds many gardeners of vanilla. The shrub grows only 50 cm or so high but spreads to well over 1 m in width. It flowers early, reaches maturity within 2 years and is quite long lived. Cherry pie may be used as a foreground shrub or as a spillover plant on top of a wall. 'Lord Roberts', with very dark purple-green leaves and deep violet flowers, is probably the most popular cultivar. Less common is 'Aureum', with yellow-lime coloured leaves and pale lavender flowers. They look attractive planted side by side.

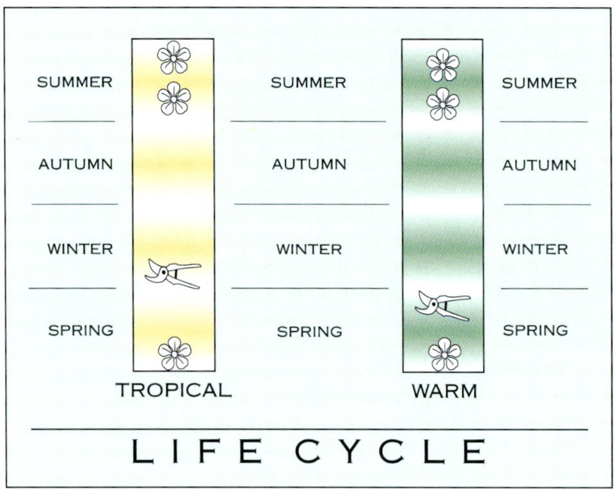

CONDITIONS

Climate Suitable for warm climates only as it is damaged by the lightest frost.

Aspect Needs a warm, sunny position sheltered from strong wind. It is best in full sun but can make do with half a day's sun.

Soil Soil should be friable and well drained. Better growth is obtained in soils enriched with well-decayed manure or compost.

GROWING METHOD

Propagation Grows easily from cuttings. Soft-tip cuttings can be taken through spring and summer while semi-hardwood cuttings are made in autumn and winter.

Watering Needs regular deep watering during the warmer months. This may need to be weekly in very hot, dry weather but can be less frequent in well-prepared soils.

Fertilising All-purpose plant food may be applied in early spring and again in midsummer.

Problems No particular pest or disease problems.

FLOWERING

Season Has a very long flowering period through spring and summer.

PRUNING

General Little pruning is needed except for shaping the bush. In early spring some of the woodier growth can be removed to make way for the new flowering shoots.

Chinese Lantern

Abutilon* x *hybridum

PRETTY, BELL-SHAPED FLOWERS in orange, yellow, white, pink or red can bloom from early spring right through autumn.

HANDSOME FOLIAGE and charming, abundant flowers—it's no wonder Chinese lantern is such a favourite with gardeners.

FEATURES

Chinese lantern is an evergreen, reasonably long-lived shrub growing between 1.5 and 2 m high, with open, bell-shaped flowers. It flowers early and matures within 2 years. Named varieties are available in white, yellow, orange, salmon, pink and red with several shades of some colours. The soft leaves are shaped like maple leaves. It is a great stand-by in the garden because of its long flowering period and good-looking foliage.

CONDITIONS

Climate Prefers warm climates but is hardy to almost freezing point.

Aspect Prefers a warm position sheltered from strong wind. Full sun is best but in warm areas tolerates dappled sunlight or half a day's sun.

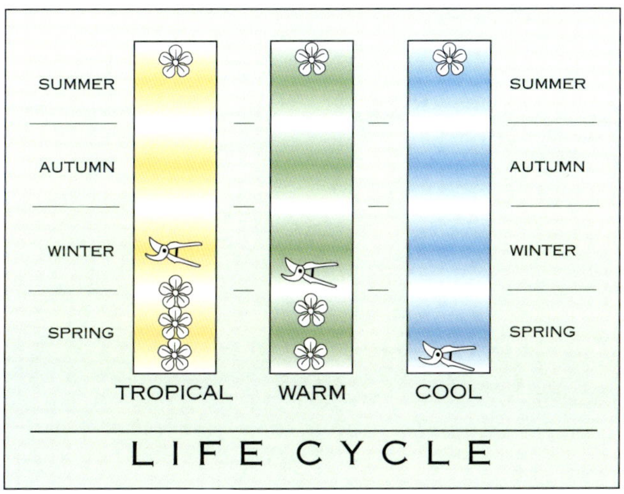

Soil Tolerates a wide range of soils but they must be well drained. Soils that have been enriched with organic matter will give the best results for this shrub.

GROWING METHOD

Propagation Early autumn is the best time to take semi-hardwood cuttings, which should root without any difficulty.

Watering Needs regular, deep watering in the warmer months but tolerates dry periods better than many shrubs.

Fertilising For best growth you should apply complete plant food during late winter and then again in midsummer.

Problems Aphids are sometimes a problem with this plant but they can be hosed off or sprayed with insecticidal soap. Leaves may be damaged by a range of leaf-chewing insects. If damage is slight, you may choose to ignore this problem, but if it is severe you may need to dust leaves with derris dust or spray the plant with a suitable insecticide.

FLOWERING

Season The main flowering flush is from early spring until early summer but plants may continue to produce a few blooms right through until the end of autumn.

PRUNING

General Plants grown in full sun should be fairly compact and need only tip pruning in late winter. Straggly plants can be cut back much harder to force new growth and a more compact shape.

Coast Rosemary

Westringia fruticosa

THE SMALL WHITE FLOWERS of the coast rosemary can be seen for most of the year. They are a perfect complement to the rather bristly foliage.

COAST ROSEMARY is here lightly clipped to emphasise its natural rounded, bushy shape.

FEATURES

This hardy, evergreen shrub is adaptable to a wide range of conditions. It tolerates salty wind, grows in arid areas, except where frosts are very severe, and once established is drought tolerant. It is a compact shrub, growing up to 2 m high and wide, with small grey-green leaves and white flowers from the first year. It matures within 2–3 years and is reasonably long lived if pruned to keep growth young. It is ideal for hedging, low screens or containers.

CONDITIONS

Climate Tolerates a wide range of conditions but not prolonged or very severe frosts.

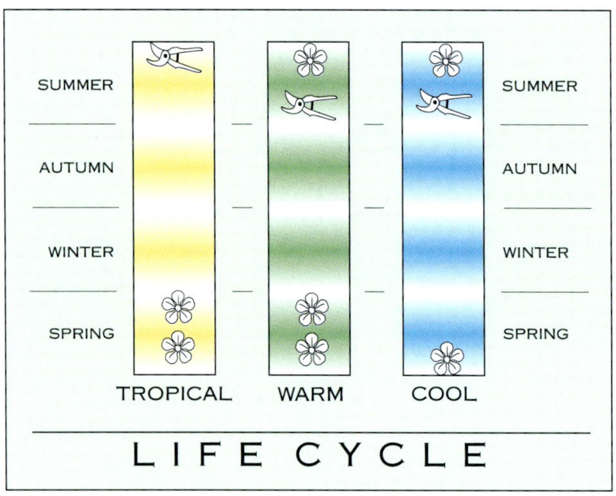

Aspect Needs full sun for good compact growth. It can be grown in windy situations and is especially useful for planting in exposed coastal areas.

Soil Must have well-drained soil. Decayed compost added well ahead of planting time helps to produce good growth.

GROWING METHOD

Propagation Soft-tip cuttings can be taken during spring and summer or semi-hardwood cuttings in late summer to autumn.

Watering Needs regular deep watering to become established but once established it will survive with only an occasional deep watering in warm, dry weather.

Fertilising Not generally necessary but a light application of blood and bone could be given during the late winter.

Problems No particular pest or disease problems. Overwet or very heavy soil may, however, induce root rot.

FLOWERING

Season The main flowering season is spring to early summer but there may be small displays of flower at other times.

PRUNING

General Cut back the bush after the main flowering has finished to maintain compact growth. Tip pruning can be carried out at almost any time of the year.

Coral Plant

Russelia equisetiformis

TUBULAR, SCARLET FLOWERS make a bright splash that lasts right through spring and summer.

ITS CASCADING HABIT makes the coral plant a great choice to grow at the top of a retaining wall. Warm climates suit it best.

FEATURES

This distinctive shrub has very slender, reed-like stems growing 1 m or more long, some upright and others arching over to the ground. Leaves are insignificant but the bright scarlet flowers appear over a long period. This reasonably long-lived plant matures within about 3 years and flowers from the first year. Coral plant is ideal for planting on banks, as a spillover plant on top of walls or simply as a filler in the garden. Because of its low maintenance requirements once established, it is an ideal plant for hard-to-get-at areas of the garden and for holiday homes. The long flowering period is another great asset.

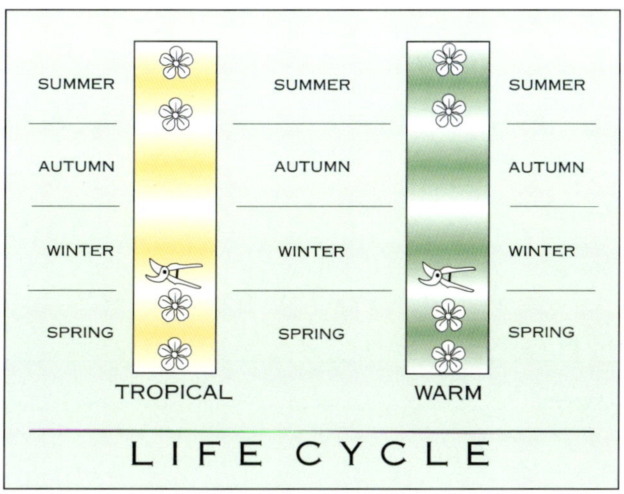

CONDITIONS

Climate Prefers warm climates where the temperature is never below freezing. It is not suitable for cool districts unless there is a very warm, sheltered micro-climate.

Aspect Must have full sun. It tolerates windy, exposed sites but looks its best where it has warmth and shelter.

Soil Must have well-drained soil but tolerates poor soils quite well.

GROWING METHOD

Propagation Semi-hardwood cuttings of the stems should strike well in warm, moist conditions.

Watering Needs regular watering to establish but once established is very drought tolerant.

Fertilising Responds well to any all-purpose plant food applied in late winter or early spring but fertilising is not absolutely necessary.

Problems No particular pest or disease problems.

FLOWERING

Season The bright coral red flowers appear in spring and may last until early autumn.

PRUNING

General Pruning is not essential but you can tip prune after flowering or in late winter just before new growth starts. Some older stems can be removed at ground level at the same time to promote growth of new flowering stems.

Cotoneaster

Cotoneaster

COTONEASTER IS GROWN for its bright scarlet berries. Here it is espaliered onto a lattice for extra stunning effect.

A DENSE HEDGE of Cotoneaster lactea *is a smart complement to the geometric veranda railing shown here.*

FEATURES

Cotoneasters range from the spreading, ground-covering *C. horizontalis* to the taller *C. lacteus* (3–4 m high) and the almost tree-like *C. pannosus*. They all produce small flowers in spring but are mainly grown for the display of bright red berries that cover these shrubs through autumn and winter. Cotoneasters take 5–10 years to maturity, depending on species and conditions, and are long lived. They flower from early in life. These hardy shrubs are very useful but don't grow them if you live near bushland—the fruits are very attractive to birds which spread the seed.

CONDITIONS

Climate Tolerant of a wide range of climates except the tropics; best in cool, moist climates.

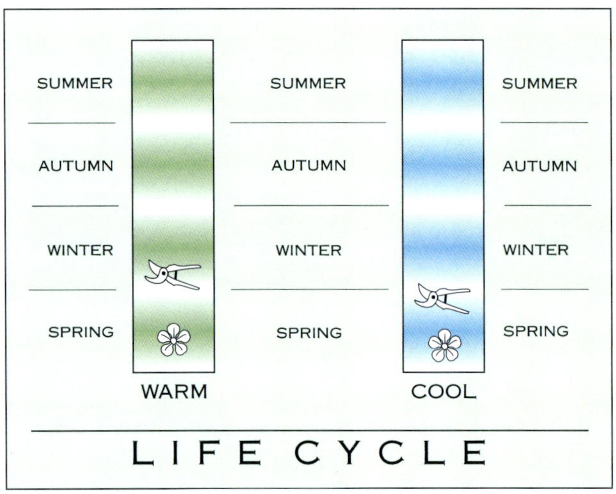

Aspect Full sun is best. Tolerates partial shade but growth there is not as dense.

Soil Tolerates poor soil but is best if grown in better quality soil that has had some organic matter added.

GROWING METHOD

Propagation Straight species are easily grown from ripe seed. Grow named varieties from semi-hardwood cuttings that are taken during the autumn months.

Watering Needs regular watering to establish but tolerates long periods without water once it is established. Maintain the plant's good appearance by occasional deep watering during dry summers.

Fertilising Fertilising is not essential but all-purpose plant food applied in early spring will give better growth. If you are growing small-leafed varieties such as *C. conspicuus* as a close-planted hedge, fertilise regularly because of the root competition between plants.

Problems No particular pest or disease problems affect these plants.

FLOWERING

Season Very small, mostly white or pinkish flowers are produced in middle to late spring.

Berries Berries are fully coloured in most species from early autumn until the middle of winter.

PRUNING

General Best carried out in late winter but can be done at other times. Whenever you prune you are likely to have fewer flowers and, therefore, fewer berries the following season.

CROTON

Codiaeum variegatum var. *pictum*

COLOURFUL CROTONS can only be grown outdoors in the tropics. Elsewhere they do well indoors.

SPECTACULAR FOLIAGE is the hallmark of these shrubs. Here, croton plants are used to create a really splendid tropical display.

FEATURES

Crotons are grown for their showy foliage, which can be splashed or spotted in a great range of patterns in yellow, orange, green, white, red and pink. The flowers are insignificant. In tropical and subtropical areas, where they can be grown outdoors, they reach 1–2.5 m in height and are a very colourful addition to the garden in massed plantings or as single specimens. Elsewhere they are often grown as indoor plants. In the tropics crotons reach maturity within 2 or 3 years. There is an enormous range of named cultivars available, giving a plethora of choice to the gardener. Apart from the amazing colour combinations and patterns, leaves may be straight, twisted or have wavy edges.

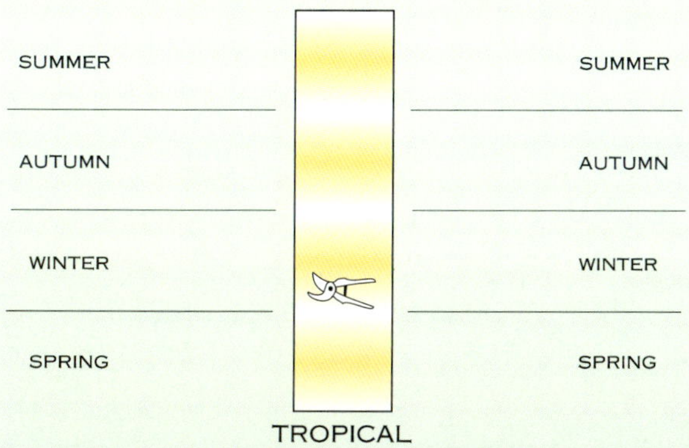

LIFE CYCLE

CONDITIONS

Climate Not suitable for cool areas. Can only be grown successfully outdoors in the tropics and in subtropical areas.

Aspect Best grown in full sun with shelter from strong wind. They tolerate some shade but the foliage colour will not be so intense if plants are grown in the shade.

Soil Must have well-drained soil enriched with compost or manure prior to planting. Use organic mulches.

GROWING METHOD

Propagation Tip cuttings of semi-hardwood are best taken in late summer and autumn.

Watering Needs regular deep watering during the warmer months but in cooler months water only when soil dries out.

Fertilising All-purpose plant food may be applied in late winter and again in midsummer.

Problems No particular insect pest or disease problems. If plants are kept too wet during the winter months, however, they will lose all or most of their leaves.

FLOWERING

Season The flowers of croton are completely insignificant, and so this plant is grown purely for the decorative foliage.

PRUNING

General Tip prune as needed to maintain the plant's bushy growth.

CROWEA

Crowea

CROWEA 'COOPER'S HYBRID' blooms generously through autumn and spring. It makes a good, reliable cut flower.

PRETTY PINK CROWEA flowers are just as much at home in a traditional European-type garden as they are in drier areas.

FEATURES

C. exalata and *C. saligna* are evergreen shrubs that blend in well with a variety of other plants. Their starry, pink-toned flowers appear early in their life and are borne over a long period. *C. exalata* grows to about 70 cm, *C. saligna* to about 1 m. Croweas mature in about 2–3 years but are short lived. They look well mass planted or with other shrubs, but they can also be grown in pots.

CONDITIONS

Climate Prefers a mild climate without frost. *C. saligna* tolerates more heat than *C. exalata*.

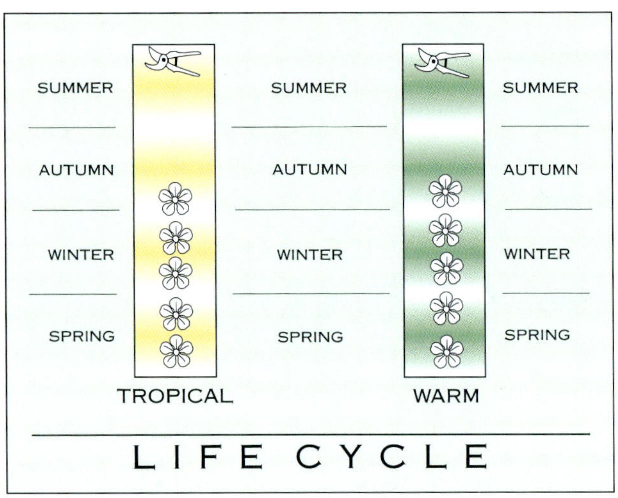

Aspect Prefers morning sun with afternoon shade or dappled sunlight and needs protection from strong wind.

Soil Soil should be sandy and well drained for best results. Well-decayed compost or leaf mould added to the soil well before planting will improve growth too.

GROWING METHOD

Propagation May be grown from seed but to maintain desirable form or flower colour grow them from semi-hardwood cuttings taken from late summer to the middle of autumn.

Watering Needs regular watering to establish. Once they are established, plants may need heavy watering every two or three weeks in the warmer months.

Fertilising A light dressing of blood and bone or a fertiliser formulated for Australian native plants may be applied in late winter. Leaf mould used as a mulch provides nutrients too.

Problems No particular pest or disease problems.

FLOWERING

Season The long blooming period runs from autumn until late spring with occasional flowers through summer. Crowea makes a good cut flower too.

PRUNING

General Light pruning after flowering helps to maintain a compact growth habit.

Daphne

Daphne

CLUSTERS OF SMALL PINK AND WHITE FLOWERS give off a truly wonderful sweet fragrance. Leaves can be variegated or plain.

DAPHNE HAS A REPUTATION for being temperamental but it is easy to give it the conditions it needs to thrive.

FEATURES

Daphnes are grown primarily for their sweet fragrance and should be planted in the garden where their perfume can be enjoyed, close to the house or beside a path. They can also be grown in containers. Individual flowers are star-shaped, mostly pink or white, and are borne in clusters on the stem ends or in leaf axils. *D.* x *burkwoodii* and *D. odora* grow about 1 m high while *D. cneorum* is rarely higher than 50 cm but may be up to 1 m wide. Daphnes mature in 5–10 years and can live for more than 20 years, but only if conditions are ideal.

CONDITIONS

Climate Not suitable for the tropics. *D.* x *burkwoodii* and *D. cneorum* prefer cool climates; *D. odora* needs a warm area.

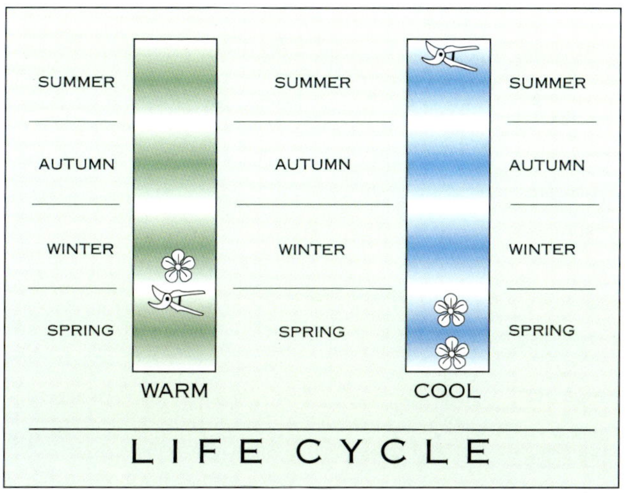

Aspect Prefers a position where it will receive morning sun and afternoon shade with shelter from strong, drying winds. Filtered sunlight is also suitable.

Soil Must have perfectly drained soil with a high organic content. Roots should be kept cool by mulching with well-decayed manure or compost but ensure that mulch is kept well clear of the stem.

GROWING METHOD

Propagation Tip cuttings taken in early summer are most likely to succeed.

Watering Deep regular watering is necessary during the warmer months but soil should never be overwet. Overwet soil for even short periods may result in root rot.

Fertilising Apply blood and bone or azalea and camellia food in early spring.

Problems Sudden death of daphnes is usually the result of root rot. They may be attacked by scale insects, which can be wiped off with a damp cloth or sprayed with white oil. There are some virus diseases of daphne for which there is no cure. Symptoms may include twisting and puckering of leaves, general stunting, yellow markings on leaves or blackening of buds.

FLOWERING

Season *D. odora* flowers through winter and sometimes into early spring. *D.* x *burkwoodii* and *D. cneorum* flower early to middle spring.

PRUNING

General Cutting sprigs of flowers for the house is probably all the pruning needed.

Diosma

Coleonema pulchrum

BRUSH AGAINST the delicate foliage of the diosma or breath of heaven and you will release a lovely, lingering scent.

SMALL, STARRY DIOSMA FLOWERS come in several shades of pink that contrast well with the fine green or yellow foliage.

FEATURES

This evergreen South African shrub grows to 1.5–2 m within about 2 years and is ideal for mixed plantings. Small flowers come in several shades of pink: to be sure of getting the one you want, buy plants in flower. A dwarf form, 'Sunset Gold', has yellowy foliage. It rarely grows more than 50 cm high and makes a fine groundcover. Both forms can be grown in pots. If conditions are right and they are kept pruned diosmas have a reasonable life span.

CONDITIONS

Climate Prefers a warm climate and must be grown in very sheltered conditions in cooler zones.

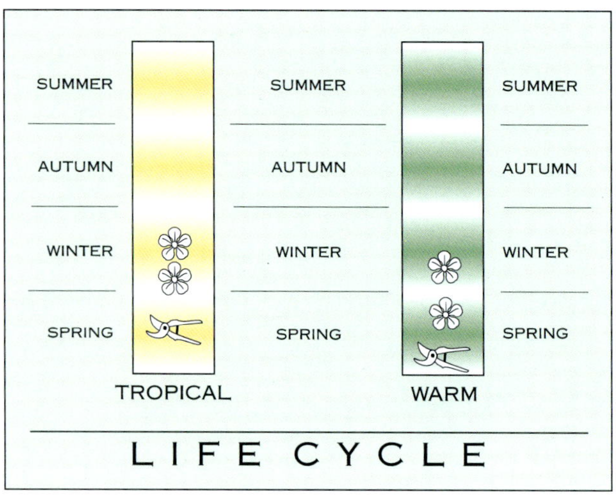

Aspect Must have full sun. Plants grown in partial shade are leggy, open and straggly.

Soil Must be grown in well-drained soil. If planted in heavy soils, bushes die quite quickly from root rots.

GROWING METHOD

Propagation Grows well from tip cuttings that have been taken from late summer until about the middle of autumn.

Watering Regular deep watering is needed to establish plants but once they are established a deep watering every two or three weeks during hot, dry weather should be sufficient to maintain the plant in good condition.

Fertilising Fertilising is not essential, but a light dressing of blood and bone or complete plant food may be applied in early spring.

Problems No particular pest or disease. Overwatering, especially if the soil is heavy, will rapidly induce root rot and this can cause the death of the plant.

FLOWERING

Season The small pink flowers are borne in great profusion from the middle of winter to the middle of spring.

PRUNING

General Prune in the middle of spring, immediately after flowering. Tip pruning can be carried out at any time during the summer months to maintain dense growth over the whole bush.

Dog Rose

Bauera rubioides

PAMPER this shy plant with its preferred conditions and be rewarded with a flush of pink flowers.

DOG OR RIVER ROSE grows to less than a metre high but spreads outwards, making it ideal for use as a groundcover or for growing in containers.

FEATURES

The dainty flowers of this shrub range in colour from deep pink to white, and so it is wise to purchase your plant while it is in bloom to get the colour you want. It prefers a slightly moist, semi-shaded position and usually grows to less than 1 m high, making it very suitable for containers. It may be short lived and reaches maturity in 2 or 3 years. Dog rose blends in well with many other plants.

CONDITIONS

Climate Not suitable for the tropics. Grows quite well in cool areas but does not tolerate heavy frost.

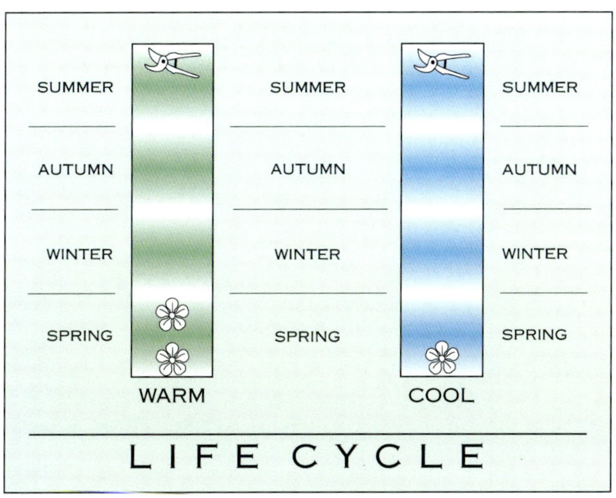

Aspect Does well in dappled sunlight or in a position where it gets some morning sun but is shaded during the hottest part of the day. Shelter from strong wind is needed, too.

Soil Prefers a sandy type of soil that does not dry out too readily. Although this shrub likes moist soils it will not do well in heavy, water-logged clays.

GROWING METHOD

Propagation Tip cuttings may be taken from late spring until late autumn.

Watering Keep the soil just moist throughout the warmer months but this does not mean daily watering is required. A good soaking once or twice a week should be sufficient if the plant is well mulched.

Fertilising Fertilising is generally not necessary but the plant may be given a light dressing of blood and bone in early spring.

Problems No specific pest or disease problems.

FLOWERING

Season The main flowering period is through spring but there may be a few flowers from time to time through the summer.

PRUNING

General Light pruning may be carried out after the main flowering flush, if so desired. If growth is uneven, the plant can be trimmed back at any time of the year.

ERIOSTEMON

Eriostemon myoporoides

ALSO KNOWN AS WAXFLOWERS, eriostemon flowers open to white from their decorative, rounded pink buds. They do, indeed, look rather waxy.

GREY-GREEN ERIOSTEMON is easy to grow in the garden or in pots, as long as the soil is well drained.

FEATURES

There are a number of species of eriostemon grown; *E. myoporoides* is the most popular. It is a rounded shrub growing about 1 m high and wide with very aromatic foliage and pale pink starry flowers. They are preceded by attractive, rounded buds that are evident for some weeks before the flowers open. Eriostemon reaches maturity within 2–3 years and, if conditions are ideal, will live for a long time. It can be grown in a mixed planting or in a pot.

CONDITIONS

Climate Needs a temperate climate and does not thrive in either the coldest areas or the tropics.

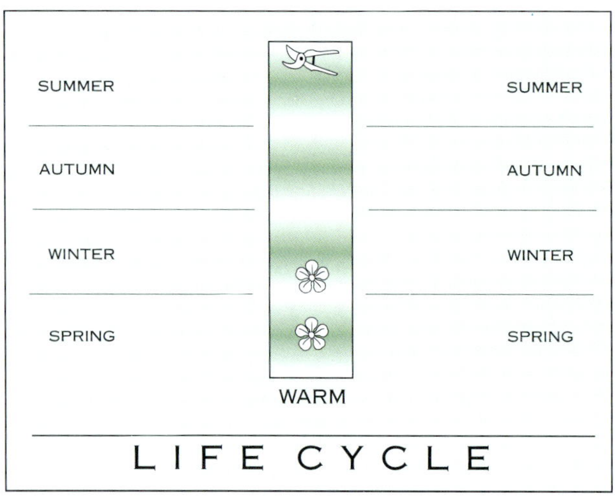

Aspect Best planted where it receives morning sun and afternoon shade, or dappled sunlight for most of the day. It prefers a position sheltered from strong wind.

Soil Soil must be well drained but it should contain plenty of humus. Well-decayed organic matter can be dug in well ahead of planting time. Apply mulch but keep it away from the stems.

GROWING METHOD

Propagation Can be grown from seed or from cuttings. Firm tip cuttings are best taken through summer and autumn.

Watering Regular deep watering is needed during the warmer months but the soil should never become waterlogged.

Fertilising Fertilising is not essential but a light dressing of blood and bone may be applied in late winter or very early spring.

Problems No particular pest or disease problems known but plants will die of root rot in heavy or overwatered soils.

FLOWERING

Season May be in bloom from late winter until the middle of spring or later, with the buds adding to the 'flowering' period.

PRUNING

General Light pruning may be done after the flowers fade. Cutting stems for indoor display may take the place of regular pruning.

ESCALLONIA

Escallonia

EVERGREEN ESCALLONIA is attractive all year round with its clusters of deep green oval leaves and sprays of long-lasting flowers.

DENSE, BUSHY ESCALLONIA is here trained against a wall to add colour throughout spring and summer.

FEATURES

Escallonia, with its attractive evergreen foliage and long-lasting flowers, should be used more often than it is. There is a great range of species and some lovely cultivars: flowers come in white and numerous shades of pink and red. Flowers appear after about 3 years and the plant grows to 2–4 m, maturing in 5–10 years. This is usually a long-lived shrub. Escallonia is a good screening or hedging plant but it can also be used as a specimen. Tolerant of strong wind, it can even be grown in exposed coastal situations. Check the tolerances of the species or cultivar you wish to grow. Many of the best cultivars were developed by Slieve Donard nurseries in Ireland.

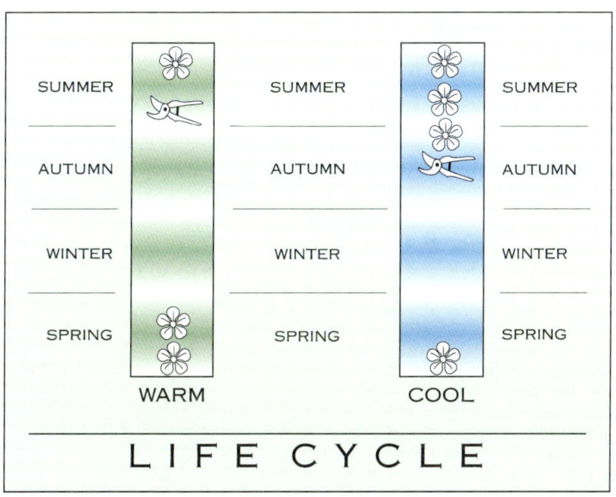

CONDITIONS

Climate Escallonias grow happily in warm to cool areas. Few tolerate very severe cold.

Aspect Needs full sun exposure for best results but is tolerant of windy sites.

Soil Needs well-drained soil but is not fussy about soil type. Escallonia grows in quite poor soils but better results are obtained in soils enriched with organic matter.

GROWING METHOD

Propagation Best grown from semi-hardwood cuttings taken in autumn.

Watering Regular deep watering is needed during the warmer months. Organic mulches help to retain moisture and increase soil fertility as they break down.

Fertilising Apply complete plant food in early spring and again in midsummer.

Problems No particular pest or disease.

FLOWERING

Season Most escallonias flower from the middle of spring until autumn although there are slight variations depending on species or cultivar.

PRUNING

General Prune immediately after flowering has finished. In cooler areas where frost may be a problem even in spring, it is best to delay pruning until the possibility of further frosts is well past.

EUPHORBIA

Euphorbia characias subspecies *wulfenii*

THE EUPHORBIA FLOWER is the small yellow centre, while the showy lime-green petals are really bracts.

AN UNUSUAL COLOUR for a cottage garden border—the fresh lime-green of euphorbia, also known as spurge, is most effective.

FEATURES

Euphorbia is valued for the contrast it provides in the garden: the foliage is very soft green and the lime green 'flowers' (really bracts) make a great foil for other colours. In good conditions it will live for 10 years or more; maturity is within 2–3 years. Growing to about 1 m high and sometimes as wide, it looks best placed in a mixed shrub border or as a background to annuals or perennials. The milky sap is caustic, and so take care when cutting these plants.

CONDITIONS

Climate As a plant of Mediterranean origin this plant tolerates all but the coldest zones.

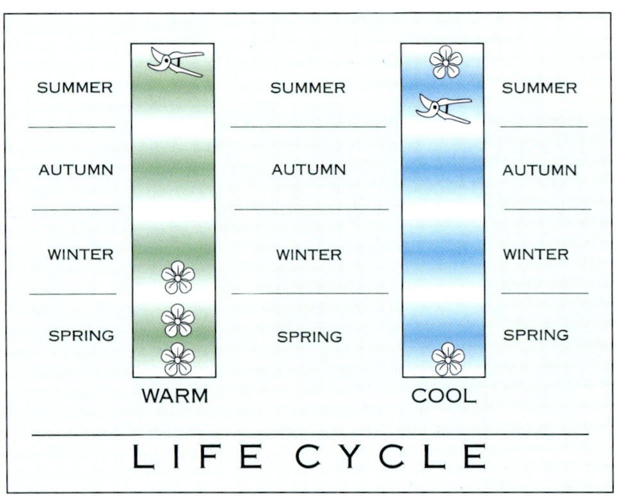

Aspect Must have full sun for best results.

Soil Tolerates quite poor soil conditions as long as it is well drained. Soils enriched with organic matter produce more vigorous growth.

GROWING METHOD

Propagation These plants often self-seed and should be transplanted when very small. Firm tip cuttings can be taken in both late summer and early autumn.

Watering Once established, this is a very drought-tolerant plant. A heavy watering every couple of weeks in warm weather should keep it in good condition.

Fertilising Fertilising is not essential but blood and bone or pelletted poultry manure may be applied either in late winter or after flowering finishes in late spring.

Problems No particular pest or disease problems.

FLOWERING

Season From late winter until late spring, later in cool areas. The actual flower is rather small but the showy lime green bracts are very striking.

Cutting This makes an unusual and attractive addition to a mixed posy. Immerse cut stems in boiling water for a few seconds to seal off the flow of milky sap.

PRUNING

General Although it is a messy job, stems should be cut back after flowering to help promote the growth of the stems that flower the next year.

Euryops

Euryops pectinatus

A WELCOME SPLASH OF WINTER COLOUR is provided by the yellow, daisy-like flowers of the euryops. Dead-head flowers regularly and this plant will bloom through spring. It will also benefit from being cut back hard after flowering has finished.

FEATURES

This neat, evergreen shrub grows to about 1 m high and wide. The leaves are covered with fine hairs, giving a grey-green effect, and the bright yellow, daisy-like flowers add colour to the garden throughout winter and into spring. Euryops will flower from the first year but it takes up to 2 years to reach maturity. With hard cutting back to keep growth fresh, plants will live a fair time but it is best to start new cuttings after about 5 years. Euryops looks well grown in a group with other shrubs or as a background plant for annuals or perennials.

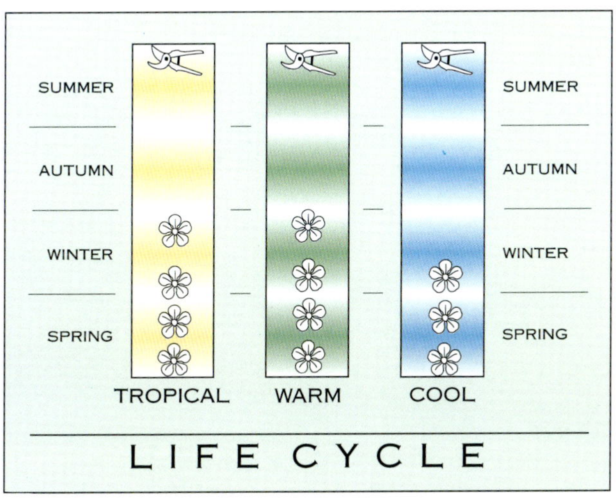

CONDITIONS

Climate Tolerates all but the coldest areas.

Aspect Must have full sun to grow and flower well.

Soil Tolerates a wide range of soils but prefers a well-drained soil.

GROWING METHOD

Propagation Strikes fairly easily from cuttings taken during the autumn months.

Watering Needs regular watering to establish, but once plants are established they cope well with dry periods. However, regular deep watering every week or two produces a healthier plant.

Fertilising Fertilising is not essential but the plant responds well to an application of complete plant food in spring and again in late summer.

Problems No particular pest or disease problems.

FLOWERING

Season Often flowers throughout winter into late spring. In some areas it may not begin flowering until late winter but it should continue until late spring.

PRUNING

General Cut back fairly hard after flowering to promote new growth from lower down the stems. Continual dead-heading will result in a much longer flowering display.

Fijian Fire Plant

Acalypha wilkesiana and cultivars

FIJIAN FIRE PLANT is valued for its strikingly patterned and coloured leaves rather than for its dull, catkin-like flower.

UNDER IDEAL CONDITIONS Fijian fire plants will flourish, reaching up to 3 m in height.

FEATURES

Fijian fire plant is grown mainly for its decorative foliage, as the flowers are not a feature. The species has leaves that may be green to reddish in colour and there are a number of very striking cultivars with a range of leaf patterns and colours. The plant is long lived, reaching maturity after about 5 years. Fijian fire plant reaches 2–3 m high, so that this shrub is an excellent background plant for warm climate gardens. It can also be mass planted to form an informal hedge. In a large tub it would make a fine feature plant on a patio or large balcony.

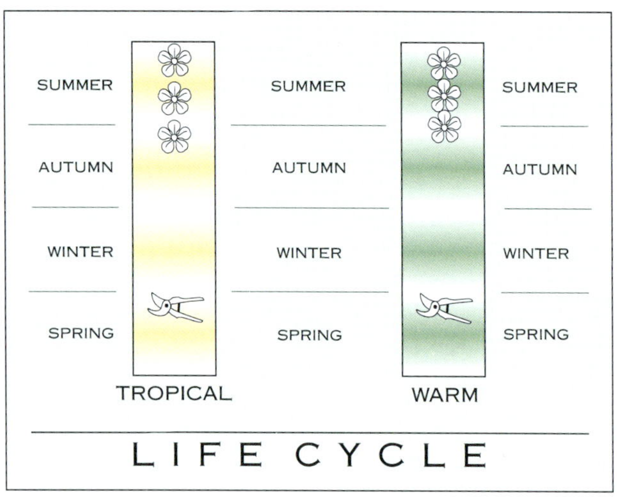

CONDITIONS

Climate Suitable only for warm, frost-free areas and does best in the tropics and subtropics.

Aspect Needs full sun to get the best foliage colour but it tolerates some shade. Although it needs shelter from strong wind, it does well in coastal gardens that are not directly exposed to salt winds.

Soil Needs well-drained soil that has been enriched with organic matter. It responds well to the use of organic mulches, too.

GROWING METHOD

Propagation Tip cuttings taken from late spring through until autumn should strike readily.

Watering Needs deep, regular watering during the warmer months.

Fertilising Apply blood and bone or complete plant food in early spring and again in midsummer.

Problems No particular pest or disease problems.

FLOWERING

Season A reddish, tassel-like catkin is produced during summer and autumn. It does not, however, add greatly to the decorative effect.

PRUNING

General Needs pruning only to maintain shape. If pruning is necessary, it should be done during early spring.

FIRETHORN

Pyracantha

SPECTACULAR AUTUMN AND WINTER DISPLAYS of bright orange berries make the firethorn popular for screening and hedges.

FIRETHORN is a large, spreading shrub with fiercely thorny stems. It can be pruned but this reduces the display of berries.

FEATURES

Grown mainly for screening and hedging, especially in cooler areas, the firethorn has glossy green leaves and thorny stems. In spring clusters of white flowers are quite attractive, and they appear from early in the life of the plant. During autumn and winter the long-lasting display of bright orange or red berries is very decorative, but they are attractive to birds, which spread the seed. It should not be grown in areas adjacent to bushland. There are several species of these shrubs, which are quite long lived. Many named cultivars are available in cool districts, where they thrive. Although mainly used for hedging, they can also be espaliered. They grow generally from 3 to 5 m high, a height they reach after 5–10 years.

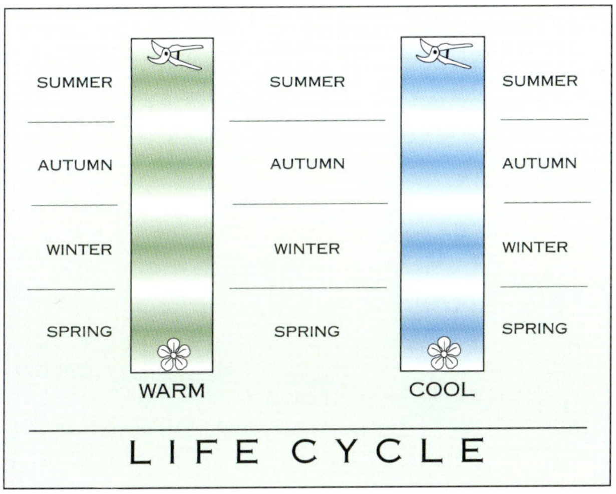

CONDITIONS

Climate Best in a cool, moist climate but grows well in most areas except the tropics.

Aspect Needs full sun for healthy, compact growth. Tolerates wind and is often grown as a windbreak or hedge.

Soil Tolerates a wide range of soil conditions. Prefers well-drained soil enriched with organic matter but this plant also grows quite well in poor soils.

GROWING METHOD

Propagation Grows readily from seed, which produces variable results. Semi-hardwood cuttings taken in autumn should strike well.

Watering Water regularly to establish. It copes well with long, dry periods but does very well when watered heavily, even if only once every two or three weeks.

Fertilising Fertilising is not essential but a complete plant food may be applied in early spring.

Problems No particular pest or disease problems.

FLOWERING

Season The clusters of white flowers appear on the bush in late spring.

Berries The colourful berry display in autumn and winter is the main reason for growing one of these shrubs.

PRUNING

General Not generally necessary. Trimming or shaping can be done at almost any time of year.

GARDENIA

Gardenia augusta

GARDENIAS ARE CHERISHED for their beautiful, strongly perfumed white flowers that darken to cream as they age.

CAREFUL POSITIONING reaps fragrant rewards: in too shady a spot blooms are poor, in too sunny they brown rapidly.

FEATURES

Gardenias, with their glossy dark green leaves and heavily scented white flowers, are among the most popular shrubs of all. There are several forms but all have white, perfumed flowers. *G. augusta* 'Radicans' is generally less than 30 cm high but may spread 1 m wide in good conditions. *G. augusta* 'Florida' grows 1–1.5 m high and has medium-sized blooms, while the variety 'Grandiflora', with larger flowers, will reach 2 m and more. There are also some named varieties with large blooms, such as 'Magnifica' and 'Professor Pucci'. These long-lived plants mature after 3–5 years but flower from the first year. Plant gardenias where their perfume can be enjoyed most, such as under a window or beside a path. They can also be used as container plants.

CONDITIONS

Climate Warm areas and tropics are best.

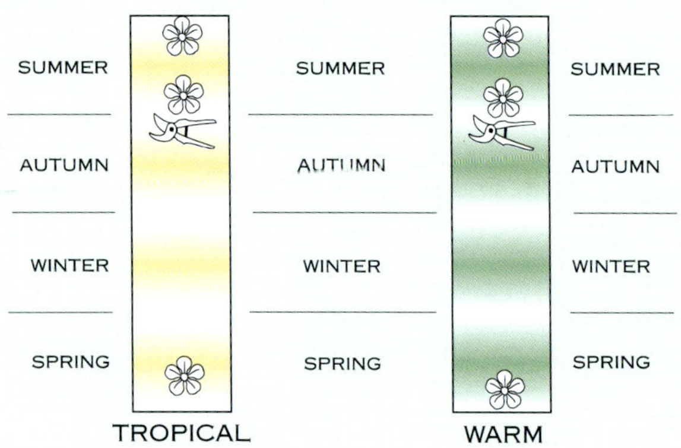

LIFE CYCLE

Aspect Needs morning sun and afternoon shade, or dappled sunlight. If it is too shady the shrub will be leggy and blooming will be poor. When gardenias get too much sun, blooms brown rapidly.

Soil Needs well-drained, slightly acid soil with plenty of added compost or manure. Mulches of decayed manure or compost should be maintained during the warmer months.

GROWING METHOD

Propagation Semi-hardwood cuttings taken in autumn give the best strike rate.

Watering Needs regular deep watering throughout the warmer months but soil should never be waterlogged or root rots will flourish.

Fertilising Apply blood and bone or azalea and camellia food in early spring and again in midsummer.

Problems Scale insects may be a problem. They may be wiped off with a damp cloth or sprayed with white oil. It is normal for many of the older leaves to turn bright yellow once or twice a year before dropping off—it is a form of self-pruning. If the new leaves are very pale with prominent green veins you should give your gardenia a dose of iron chelates.

FLOWERING

Season The main flowering flush is during late spring and early summer but there may be blooms appearing throughout the summer months.

PRUNING

General Tip pruning can be carried out immediately after flowering. If your gardenia has long bare stems with tip growth only, cut back half the stems to the desired height then wait until you see new growth coming from the base before cutting the remaining stems.

Geraldton Wax

Chamelaucium uncinatum

LOVELY, WAXY FLOWERS in white or pink are excellent whether cut for the vase or left on the shrub to form a focus point in the garden.

GERALDTON WAX thrives in a sloping, sunny position in the garden, making a graceful, arching shrub.

FEATURES

A shrub of very open habit that grows from 2 to 3 m high, Geraldton wax is popular for its long-lasting floral display which provides excellent cut flowers as well as attractive garden decoration. Flowers may be in various shades of pink or white. Short-lived in poor conditions, they can last for many years if conditions suit. Maturity is reached in about 3 years. There are a number of cultivated varieties available, and so plants should be bought in bloom. The foliage is aromatic when rubbed or crushed.

CONDITIONS

Climate Not suitable for the tropics or the coldest zones as it is not frost tolerant. Grows best in warm, moderate climates with low humidity.

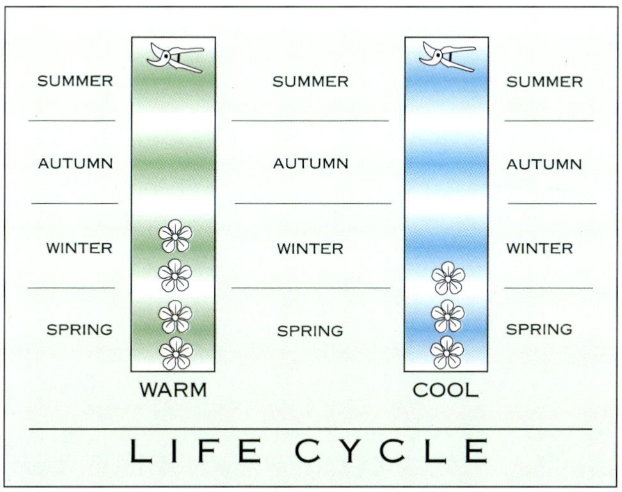

Aspect Best in full sun all day but tolerates half a day's sun. Good air circulation is very important too, and so it is an advantage to grow it on sloping ground.

Soil Must have perfectly drained soil and prefers sandy or gravelly soils. Raised beds may need to be made if there is any doubt at all about the drainage.

GROWING METHOD

Propagation Tip cuttings of firmer growth can be taken from early summer until early autumn.

Watering Regular deep watering is needed for establishment but soil should not be waterlogged at any time. Once established, this plant can survive on occasional heavy watering during the warm months.

Fertilising Little or no fertiliser is needed. A light application of pelletted poultry manure or blood and bone may be applied in spring.

Problems No particular insect or disease problems. These plants succumb to root rot very readily if the soil conditions are heavy and wet, or if mulch is allowed to build up around the stem of the plant.

FLOWERING

Season The shrub is covered in flowers from winter through until late spring.

Cutting Geraldton wax is a long-lasting cut flower.

PRUNING

General When cutting for the house or tip pruning after flowering never cut into the older wood or you will kill the plant. Tip pruning does, however, help to encourage bushy growth.

GREVILLEA

Grevillea

UNUSUAL PROJECTING STIGMAS give the grevillea flower its nickname of the spider flower. It comes in every colour but blue.

GREVILLEAS ARE SUITABLE for all climates. Most, like this flourishing 'Moonlight', thrive in full sun sheltered from wind.

FEATURES

There are well over 200 species of grevillea and many species and cultivars are grown as ornamental shrubs. They range from low groundcovers such as *G. laurifolia* to very tall trees such as the silky oak, *G. robusta*. Popular types include 'Robyn Gordon', 'Honey Gem', 'Misty Pink', 'Moonlight' and 'Ned Kelly'. Leaves may be finely divided or lobed, and the intricately shaped flowers may be red, pink, cream, yellow, burnt orange or white, depending on variety. Many grevilleas reach maturity in 3–5 years, and they can be reasonably long lived if cut back regularly. Grevilleas are very attractive to birds. They have many uses, some as screens or hedges.

CONDITIONS

Climate Depends on species. Some thrive in very warm areas, others are at home in the coldest areas. Consult your local nursery for a suitable type.

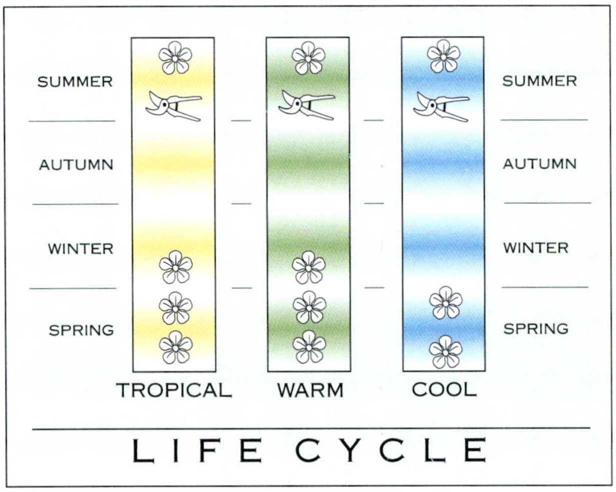

Aspect The vast majority of grevilleas need to be in full sun but there are a few species that prefer light shade. These species are more likely to be grown by specialists.

Soil Well-drained soil is a must, although most grevilleas tolerate quite poor soil. However, grevilleas come from a wide range of climates and environments and it is a good idea to check the preferred conditions of each before you buy it.

GROWING METHOD

Propagation Species can be grown from seed but grow the cultivated varieties from semi-hardwood cuttings taken in late summer and autumn.

Watering They need regular deep watering to establish but once established tolerate dry periods well. Occasional deep watering in a very dry summer is beneficial.

Fertilising It is best not to use any fertiliser at all. A mulch of leaf litter or very well-decayed compost provides the little nutrient they need.

Problems Webbing caterpillars and borers can sometimes be a problem. Check your plants closely several times a year and remove damage by hand. A fungal leaf disease known as grevillea scorch may occur in humid, showery conditions; spraying with copper oxychloride should prevent it from getting worse.

FLOWERING

Season Most have their main flowering flush from late winter until early summer with intermittent flowers at other times.

PRUNING

General Regular tip pruning as flowers fade will make plants more compact and keep them producing fresh young growth.

HAKEA

Hakea

THE UNUSUAL SHAPE of the Hakea laurina *flower gives it its apt common names of the pincushion or sea-urchin flower.*

HAKEA LAURINA, *like most hakeas, does best in a warm climate. It can be grown as a shrub or trained as a small tree.*

FEATURES

Many of the spectacular flowering shrubby hakeas are suitable for growing only in areas of low humidity as they do not tolerate humidity and summer rainfall. The showiest species have dense racemes or clusters of flowers in pink, red, yellow, orange or white. Less spectacular but useful species such as *H. salicifolia* have clusters of cream or white spidery flowers in the leaf axils. *H. salicifolia*, growing from 4 m to 6 m high, is an excellent screening plant and *H. laurina*, also 4–6 m high, is sometimes used as a tall shrub or small tree in street plantings. Hakeas come from a wide range of habitats, and so check to see if they suit your situation. Their life span varies according to the species and the growing conditions, but most flower from about 3 years and reach maturity between 5 and 10 years. In flower they are very attractive to birds.

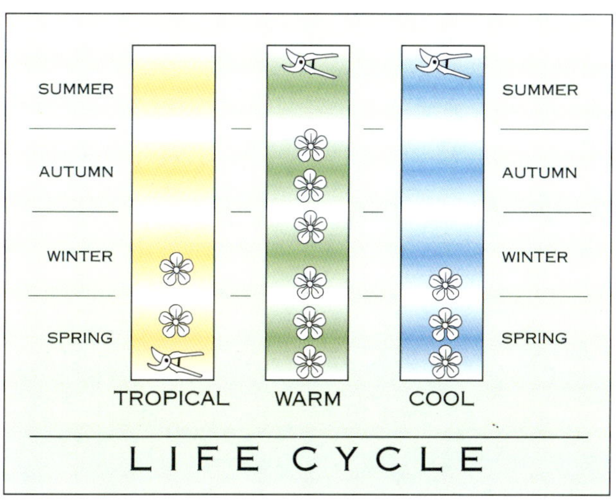

CONDITIONS

Climate Depends on species chosen. Many of the best types in flower need a Mediterranean climate with wet winters and dry summers. Most prefer a warm climate.

Aspect As they come from a wide range of habitats some prefer full sun while others tolerate light shade. Very heavy shade is not suitable.

Soil Prefers well-drained sandy or gravelly soil. *H. salicifolia* tolerates clay soils but not if they remain waterlogged after rain or irrigation.

GROWING METHOD

Propagation Best grown from seed as cuttings are difficult. The woody seed case (follicle) can be taken from the plant and kept in a warm, sunny spot until the seeds are released. They can then be sown fresh and should germinate within three or four weeks.

Watering Needs regular watering to establish but once plants are established they tolerate long dry periods very well.

Fertilising Do not fertilise hakeas.

Problems No special insect pest or disease problems but overwatering, especially in heavier soils, will induce root rot.

FLOWERING

Season Many hakeas flower from late winter throughout spring. Some, such as *H. laurina*, flower earlier, from autumn until about the middle of winter.

PRUNING

General Prune lightly after flowering to keep bushes compact and neat.

Hawthorn

Crataegus

ABUNDANT, SCENTED WHITE BLOSSOMS appear on the hawthorn in spring and are followed by bright red berries in autumn and winter.

HAWTHORN is the traditional English hedgerow shrub but it grows well in any cool, moist area.

FEATURES

Mostly grown as hedging or screening plants, hawthorns can be regarded as tall shrubs or small trees. They are deciduous, with shapely lobed leaves. Masses of white blossom in spring are followed by bright red berries that may persist after leaf fall. Stems are very spiny, which explains their use as hedgerows in Britain and the United States. Heights may be from 4 to 7 m but plants are commonly kept to 3 or 4 m. Long lived, they take about 3 years to flower and 5–10 years to mature.

CONDITIONS

Climate Not suitable for the tropics. They perform best in cooler, moist climates where autumn colour is brightest but do quite well in warm districts.

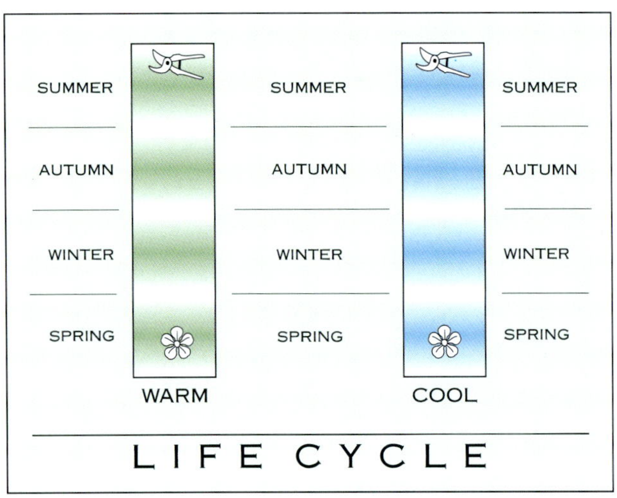

Aspect These plants tolerate wind and are best planted in full sun.

Soil Although they prefer deep, well-drained soils they perform quite well in a wide range of different soil types.

GROWING METHOD

Propagation Species may be grown from seed from cleaned berries but the seed needs several months of chilling (below 4 degrees Celsius) to break dormancy. Named varieties are propagated by grafting or budding.

Watering Regular deep watering produces the best plants but once established hawthorns tolerate dry periods better than many other cool climate plants.

Fertilising Apply complete plant food in late winter or early spring, but plants can survive without supplementary feeding.

Problems No particular pest or disease problems.

FLOWERING

Season Hawthorns produce abundant flowers in spring. The whole shrub appears to be smothered in white blossom.

Berries Bright red berries appear on hawthorn plants in autumn and winter.

PRUNING

General If used for hedging, hawthorns should be pruned after flowering although this will reduce or eliminate the display of berries. At this time thin, tangled growth can be cut out of the centre, too, but wear sturdy gloves and protective sleeves as the thorns can be vicious.

HEATH

Erica

SMALL, NEEDLE-LIKE LEAVES and bell-shaped or tubular flowers are typical of heath.

CHOOSE SPECIES CAREFULLY and heath gives colour practically all year round. Here several varieties are set off by yellow Calluna *flowers.*

FEATURES

This large group of shrubs is native to Europe and South Africa, and ranges in height from less than half a metre to 3 m tall. Flowers are tubular or bell-shaped in white, pink, violet, coral, crimson and bicolours. Unless conditions are ideal they are short lived, maturing after 3–5 years. Heaths are a challenge to grow because of their soil and climatic requirements but they can be used as groundcovers, in massed plantings and some in rockeries.

CONDITIONS

Climate Not suitable for the tropics, hot arid areas or humid coastal ones. They are best in cool areas with low humidity.

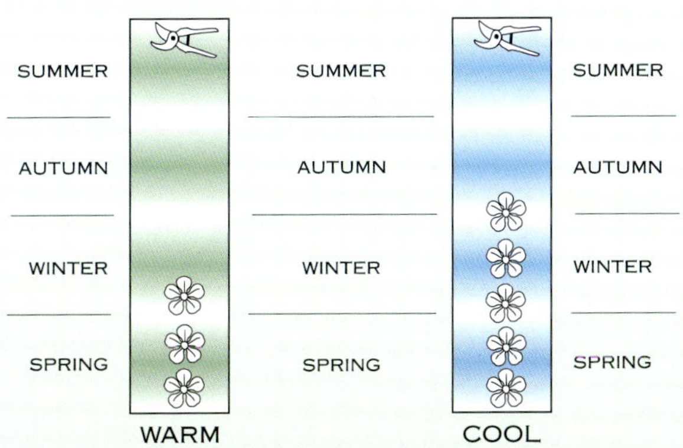

LIFE CYCLE

Aspect Must have full sun and good air circulation. Do not crowd plants as this creates a humid atmosphere around them.

Soil These shrubs need soil that is very well drained but has a high organic content to retain some moisture during dry periods. This is very hard to achieve. Mulching with gravel or pebbles helps retain moisture without creating extra humidity around the plant.

GROWING METHOD

Propagation Grow from tip cuttings of semi-hardwood taken during autumn or very early winter.

Watering Needs regular deep watering in hot weather but soil should never be soggy.

Fertilising Little or no fertiliser is needed. If the soil is very poor you could lightly fertilise with blood and bone or azalea and camellia food during early spring.

Problems Heath plants will quickly succumb to root rot in heavy or overwet soils. In areas of high humidity and summer rainfall plants may collapse quite rapidly.

FLOWERING

Season Flowering season varies according to the species chosen. Many species flower from late winter throughout spring but others flower through autumn and winter too.

PRUNING

General Tip pruning should be carried out after flowering has finished. Never cut into the older wood.

HIBISCUS

Hibiscus rosa-sinensis

BRILLIANTLY COLOURED Hibiscus rosa-sinensis*—flowers last for just one day but beautiful new blooms will open the next morning.*

THE HAWAIIAN VERSIONS of hibiscus are notable for their enormous flowers and compact growth.

FEATURES

This evergreen shrub, also known as Chinese hibiscus, is one of the most popular of all flowering shrubs for gardens in warm areas. Heights range from about 2 m to nearly 4 m. They are long lived, reaching maturity after 5–10 years but flowering from the first year. Hibiscus can be grown as specimen shrubs, hedges, screens or in mixed plantings. The very showy flowers may be single or double and come in every colour of the rainbow.

CONDITIONS

Climate Not suitable for cold zones. Best in the tropics and other warm districts.

Aspect Needs warmth and full sun exposure for best growth and flowering.

Soil Soil should be well-drained and enriched with copious amounts of well-decayed manure or compost prior to planting. Mulch heavily with organic matter so as to maintain high humus content in the soil.

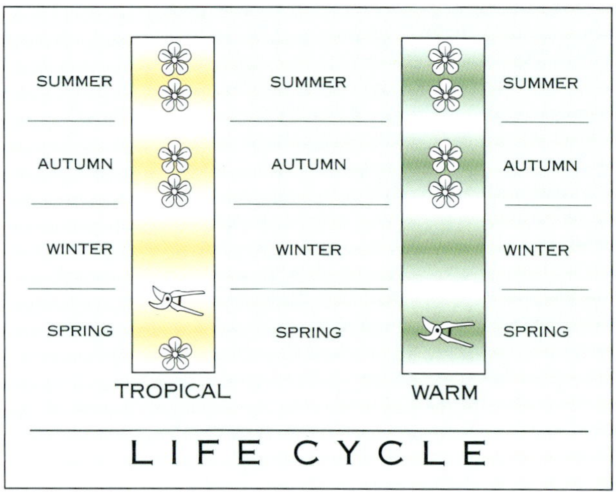

GROWING METHOD

Propagation Strikes readily from semi-hardwood cuttings taken in late summer and autumn.

Watering During the warmer months water heavily about once a week or more frequently if soil is light and sandy. During winter water every three or four weeks if weather is dry.

Fertilising Hibiscus are heavy feeders: as well as mulching, fertilise with complete plant food regularly from spring until early autumn.

Problems Aphids may attack the new growth; hose them off every couple of days. Holes in leaves are usually caused by tiny snails, crickets, caterpillars or leaf-eating beetles. Hibiscus beetles often seen in the flowers are primarily nectar and pollen feeders although they may cause holes in flowers. They are not generally responsible for bud drop. Bud drop occurs when plants have not been sufficiently watered and fertilised. It can also happen on plants that are overwatered. There is a fungal leaf disease that occurs on shrubs growing in damp or too shady situations: the only remedy is to move the plant or improve conditions.

FLOWERING

Season From late spring or early summer until the weather gets cool in late autumn or winter. With such a huge range of flowers to choose from, it is best to select your plant in bloom at the nursery. Some of the Hawaiian hybrids have extremely large flowers if growing conditions are good.

PRUNING

General Wait until spring to prune. Some varieties can be cut back by about a third while others are best tip pruned only. Be guided by observing the vigour and growth habit of your plant: if it is very vigorous you may prune more heavily.

Hibiscus

Hibiscus syriacus

THE DELIGHTFUL SUMMER-BLOOMING FLOWERS can be pink, white, crimson or lilac, like this spectacular version here.

THIS DECIDUOUS HIBISCUS (also known as shrub althea or the Syrian rose) is the hibiscus to choose if you live in cooler areas.

FEATURES

Also known as shrub althea, this long-lived, deciduous hibiscus grows 3 m or more high. It flowers in the first year but takes 5–10 years to reach maturity. *H. syriacus* is not suited to tropical areas but does well in warm and cool to cold zones. Flowers are single or double and range in colour from white, pink and mauve, to red or bicolours, mostly with a deep crimson eye in the centre. These hibiscus are best bought when in flower as there is a great range of varieties from which to choose. *H. syriacus* may be grown as an informal hedge or as a single specimen plant.

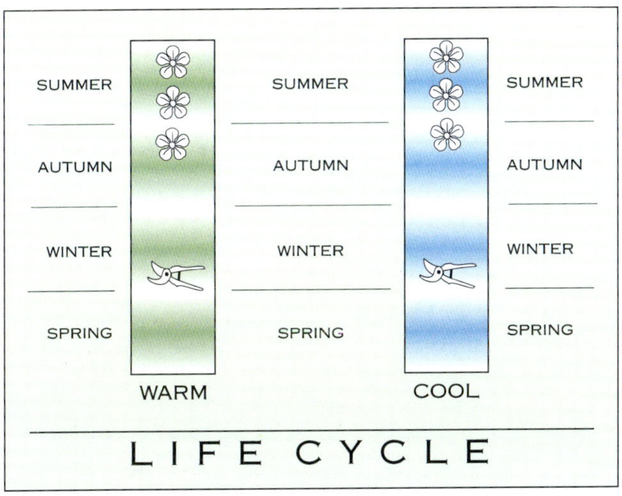

CONDITIONS

Climate Suits warm and cold areas well. Unsuitable for the tropics.

Aspect Prefers full sun to achieve its best development and flowering.

Soil Needs well-drained soil. Although it tolerates poorer soils, better results will be had from soil that has been enriched with organic matter.

GROWING METHOD

Propagation Grows easily from hardwood cuttings of dormant wood taken in winter.

Watering Needs regular watering to establish. Once established, it tolerates long, dry periods very well but when water is short both flowers and leaves will be very small.

Fertilising Apply all-purpose plant food in spring and again in midsummer.

Problems No particular insect pest or disease.

FLOWERING

Season From early summer until autumn.

PRUNING

General May need pruning to half of its growth in the first two or three years. Established plants are probably best reduced by about a third of their size. Crossing growth should be cut out of the centre of the plant. Prune in late winter while plant is still dormant.

HONEY-MYRTLE

Melaleuca

HONEY-MYRTLE IS A QUICK-GROWING SHRUB, some species of which can look like trees when mature. Here Melaleuca armillaris *is planted as a very effective windbreak on a golf course but it is useful for screening in the garden too.*

FEATURES

Honey-myrtles are the shrubby forms of the *Melaleuca* genus while the tall trees of the genus are known as paperbarks. Honey-myrtles are evergreen with a range of leaf colours and forms, and with fine 'bottlebrush'-type flowers in cream, yellow, violet, pink and red. The flowers are very attractive to birds. Honey-myrtles are reasonably long lived if they are pruned regularly. They take 3–10 years to reach maturity, depending on the species, but begin to flower early in their life. Some species, such as *M. armillaris* (4 m or more tall) are widely used as screening plants. Other commonly grown species are *M. incana*, which has fine, grey, weeping foliage, *M. nesophila*, which has violet flowers fading to white, and the red-flowered *M. hypericifolia*, which adapts to either dry or wet soils. Some species occur in exposed coastal conditions, too.

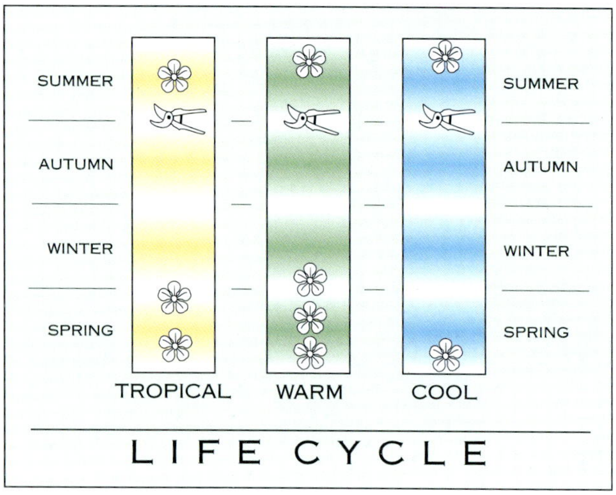

CONDITIONS

Climate Depends on species chosen. Many honey-myrtles prefer warm climates but some species thrive in the colder zones.

Aspect Needs full sun for best growth.

Soil Most prefer good drainage but some honey-myrtles, such as *M. hypericifolia*, tolerate wet or poorly drained soils.

GROWING METHOD

Propagation May be grown from seed or cuttings. Woody seed capsules placed in a paper bag in the sun will release the seed, which can be sown in spring. Semi-hardwood cuttings are best taken in late summer and autumn.

Watering Needs regular watering to establish but once it is established it tolerates long, dry periods quite well.

Fertilising Not generally needed but if desired a light dressing of blood and bone could be applied in early spring.

Problems Webbing caterpillars can be a nuisance as they mat together stems and leaves. Cut them off or remove them with a gloved hand. Check plants several times a year. Paperbark sawflies can defoliate these shrubs in late summer/early autumn. Pick them off the plants where possible or spray with pyrethrins or maldison.

FLOWERING

Season Flowering time depends on species chosen.

PRUNING

General Light pruning immediately after flowering helps maintain compact growth and should help to produce more flowers.

Honeysuckle

Lonicera

DISTINCTIVE AND FRAGRANT, honeysuckle flowers are a wonderful way to bring perfume to the garden.

THE GIANT HONEYSUCKLE Lonicera hildebrandiana *comes from Burma. It is a vast grower, not recommended for small gardens.*

FEATURES

There are a number of shrubby honeysuckles with fragrant flowers but without the rampant growth habit of the common honeysuckle vine. If pruned regularly, they are reasonably long lived, reaching maturity in 3–5 years with flowers from the first year. *L. fragrantissima* is a semi-deciduous, multi-stemmed shrub growing to almost 3 m high. It is useful for screens or background planting. *L.* x *heckrottii,* halfway between a climber and a shrub, is easily trained as a shrub 1.5 to 2 m high. It can be grown alone or in mixed plantings.

CONDITIONS

Climate Suitable for cool to warm areas but not tropics.

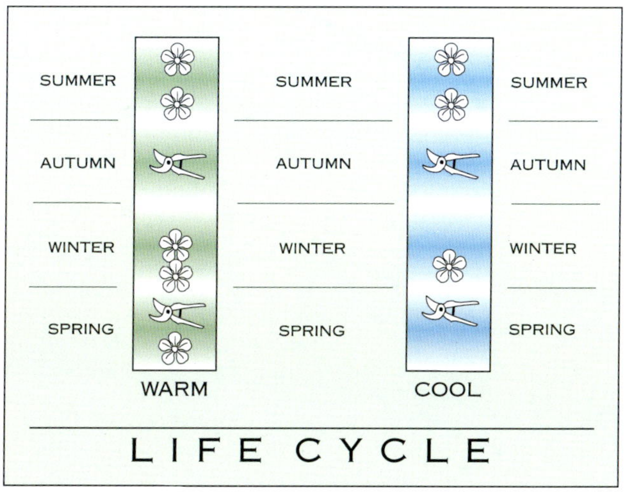

Aspect Needs full sun for best growth and flowering.

Soil Easy to grow even in poor soils but prefers well-drained soil with some organic matter added to it.

GROWING METHOD

Propagation Semi-hardwood cuttings taken in late summer and autumn should strike readily.

Watering Needs regular watering to establish but once it is established it tolerates dryness for quite long periods. However, better foliage and flowers result from giving deep, regular waterings in dry, warm weather.

Fertilising Can get along without supplementary fertiliser but benefits from a dressing of all-purpose plant food given in early spring and again during midsummer.

Problems No particular insect pest or disease problems.

FLOWERING

Season *L. fragrantissima* produces its small, cream, heavily scented flowers from the middle of winter until early spring. The pinky red and cream flowers of *L.* x *heckrottii* appear in middle spring and continue through most of the summer months.

PRUNING

General Best pruned immediately after flowering has finished. Older canes of *L. fragrantissima* should be cut out at ground level and the newer canes shortened. *L.* x *heckrottii* can be pruned to create a better shape or for directional growth.

Hydrangea

Hydrangea macrophylla

EVER POPULAR, hydrangea is a native of Korea and Japan. Ensure pink flowers by adding lime to the soil in spring, for blue flowers add aluminium sulphate.

LARGE, SHOWY, ROUND HEADS make wonderfully decorative cut flowers.

FEATURES

The large, rounded heads of hydrangea flowers make a great show in the garden throughout the summer months. Flowers may be pink, blue, white or red with many in-between tones. This long-lived, deciduous shrub grows from 50 cm to 2 m high, reaching maturity within 3–5 years. Flowers appear from early in the life of the plant. Hydrangeas make ideal background plantings and are often used to disguise fences. Lacecaps are another popular form of this hydrangea. Among other species of hydrangea well worth growing are *H. quercifolia*, with large lobed leaves and trusses of rich cream flowers, and *H. paniculata*, which grows to 4 m or more and also has creamy white flowers.

CONDITIONS

Climate Tolerates a wide range of climates but prolonged severe cold may damage plants.

Aspect Prefers dappled sunlight or morning sun and afternoon shade. Shelter from strong wind is desirable for these plants.

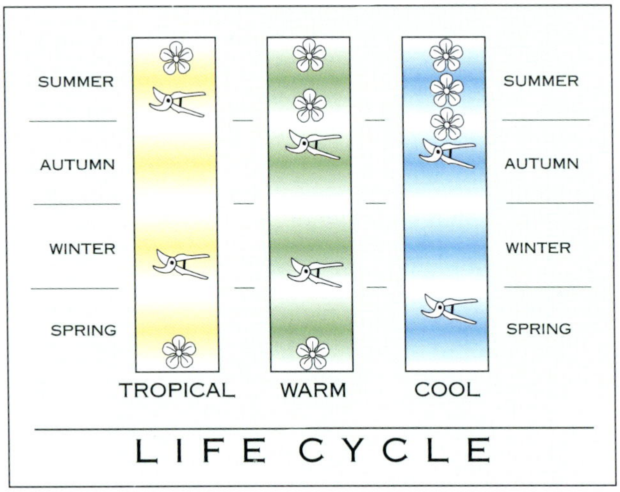

Soil Needs well-drained soil with a high content of organic matter. Dig copious quantities of well-decayed manure or compost into the ground well ahead of planting time. Plants should also be heavily mulched with similar material.

GROWING METHOD

Propagation Can be grown from soft-tip cuttings taken in spring or summer or from hardwood cuttings taken during the dormant winter period.

Watering Should not be short of water in warm months; prefers deep watering to light sprinkling.

Fertilising Apply complete plant food in early spring and again in late summer, or once blooms are over.

Problems May be attacked by hydrangea scale, which resembles blobs of toothpaste on the leaves. This should be treated by spraying with white oil. Powdery mildew shows up initially as grey-white patches on the leaves. Once the disease has progressed, leaves may show dead or dark discoloured patches. Spray with sulphur if weather is not too hot, otherwise use a fungicide registered for this disease.

FLOWERING

Season From late spring until late summer, longer when plants are grown in sheltered, cool spots.

Cutting Excellent cut flower. Cut stems early in the morning and plunge them into deep water for a few hours before arranging. Remove from the base of the stem a thick sliver of the outer covering to aid in water uptake.

PRUNING

General Cut back stems that have flowered straight after blooms fade. Leave unflowered growth alone to produce next season's flowers. Cut back old, overgrown bushes hard in late winter or early spring; remove old canes at ground level, especially from centre of the plant. You may have few flowers the next season but the following year should see overall blooming.

INDIAN HAWTHORN

Raphiolepis indica

INDIAN HAWTHORN comes from China and has no thorns, despite its name. It is popular because it is so easy to grow, thriving even in seaside gardens.

MASSES OF FLOWERS make a magnificent spring display. They look rather like apple blossom.

FEATURES

Indian hawthorn is a long-lived, evergreen shrub that grows to 2– 3 m high. It bears lovely star-shaped white flowers touched with crimson at the base of the petals, while the dark green foliage looks attractive even when the plant is not in flower. Indian hawthorn flowers early in its life and takes between 5 and 10 years to reach maturity. It is a trouble-free shrub that is often used as an informal hedge or screen. Tolerant of wind and quite harsh conditions, it is suitable for gardens in a wide range of climates and is often used in seaside gardens, although not in the front line of salt wind exposure. *R.* x *delacourii*, a hybrid between *R. indica* and *R. umbellata*, has pretty pink flowers.

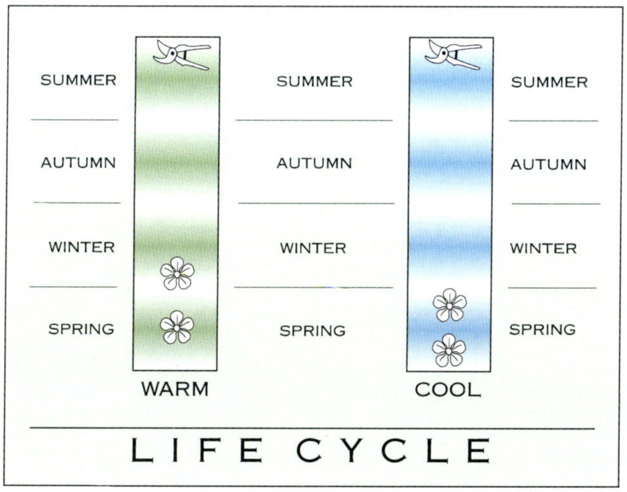

CONDITIONS

Climate Unsuitable for the tropics but it does well in cool or warm zones.

Aspect A position in full sun produces the most compact growth. Plants grown in too much shade may be sparse and leggy.

Soil Needs well-drained soil. Prefers lighter sandy soils enriched with some organic matter.

GROWING METHOD

Propagation Can be grown from seed planted in autumn. Seed should be removed from the ripe blue-black berries and cleaned before sowing. Semi-hardwood cuttings can be taken in autumn.

Watering Regular deep watering through the warmer months produces the best looking plants but it does tolerate dry periods better than some other shrubs.

Fertilising Apply complete plant food in early spring. A mulch of decayed manure or compost improves growing conditions and adds small amounts of nutrients to the soil.

Problems No particular pest or disease problems.

FLOWERING

Season From late winter until the middle of spring.

Berries The blue-black berries ripen in autumn and persist until winter.

PRUNING

General Not generally necessary. Light tip pruning for shaping could be carried out straight after flowering, if desired.

Indigo Plant

Indigofera decora

THE BRIGHTLY TINTED, pea-shaped flowers of the indigo plant are followed by long pods from which seed can easily be saved.

HANGING SPRAYS of flowers make the indigo plant look like a dwarf, pink-flowered wisteria but—alas—without the scent.

FEATURES

Growing less than 1 m high, this multi-stemmed shrub spreads by suckers, by which it is constantly renewed. It reaches a mature shape in 1–2 years and over time can form quite large clumps, although it may die down to the base in winter in all but the warmest districts. The attractive flowers are pea-shaped in a mix of bright pink, mauve and white. They appear early in the life of the shrub.

CONDITIONS

Climate Best in warm areas but it is not suitable for growing in the tropics.

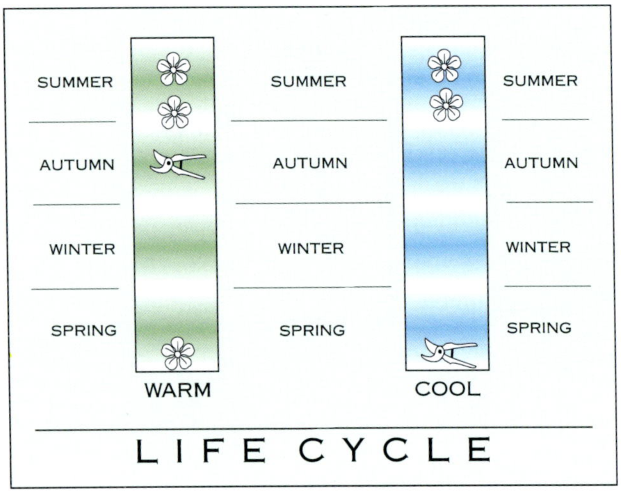

Aspect Prefers full sun but tolerates a position where there is direct sun for half a day.

Soil Not fussy about soil but soil should be well drained. Growth is very vigorous if soil is enriched with organic matter.

GROWING METHOD

Propagation Can be grown from seed sown as soon as pods are ripe. Semi-hardwood cuttings may be taken in late summer and autumn.

Watering Needs regular deep watering, about once a week, during the spring and summer.

Fertilising Fertilising is not essential but complete plant food may be applied in early spring.

Problems No particular pest or disease problems.

FLOWERING

Season The 'pea' type flowers are produced from the middle of spring until summer. The flowers combine a mixture of bright pink and white with lavender markings.

PRUNING

General May be cut back after flowering (in cool areas in spring) or left to produce seed pods. If suckers are too numerous they can be dug up or cut off with a sharp spade and discarded.

HINT

Position Grow indigo plant at the front of a mixed border or among annuals and perennials.

IXORA

Ixora chinensis

ALSO KNOWN AS jungle geranium, ixora is notable for its large clusters of flowers, that range in colour from this deep orange-red to yellow.

CHEERFUL CORAL RED FLOWERS and glossy leaves make ixora ideal for container growing.

FEATURES

Ixora is an evergreen shrub with glossy green leaves growing up to 2 m high in tropical regions but much less in other areas. Flowers in the species are red but the cultivar 'Prince of Orange' is the most frequently grown form: it has orange to coral red flowers. In the right conditions, it is a reasonably long-lived shrub and reaches maturity in 3–5 years. It flowers from early in its life. Ixora looks effective mass planted in a large garden but is also attractive grown in a mixed shrub border. It makes a good container plant, too.

CONDITIONS

Climate Quite unsuitable for cool zones. Needs a tropical or warm climate.

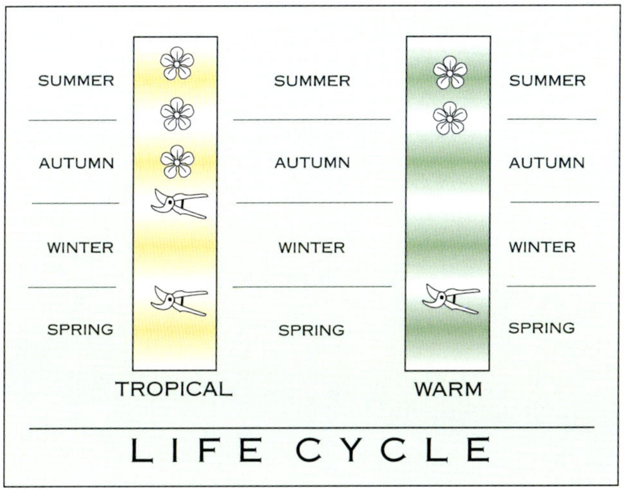

Aspect Must have warmth and shelter from wind. Prefers morning sun and afternoon shade, or dappled sunlight all day.

Soil Must have well-drained soil that contains plenty of organic matter. Dig in compost or manure well ahead of planting time. The plant should also be mulched.

GROWING METHOD

Propagation Strike from tip cuttings taken in spring. It is essential to maintain humidity around the cuttings until they are well rooted.

Watering This plant needs regular deep watering during the warmer months. During cool weather you should allow the soil to dry out somewhat between waterings.

Fertilising Apply blood and bone or complete plant food once during early spring and then once again in midsummer.

Problems No specific insect pest or disease problems. However, overwet or heavy soils will cause root rot. New growth and flowers will burn if exposed to very hot sun or strong wind.

FLOWERING

Season Long flowering period through the summer and autumn months.

Berries Black berries follow the flowers.

PRUNING

General May be pruned immediately after flowers fade to remove spent blooms or pruned by about a third in late winter or very early spring. The heavier pruning is carried out on older, mature plants only.

JAPONICA

Chaenomeles speciosa

FLOWERING BRANCHES of japonica look elegant indoors and last very well in water. Flowers also come in dramatic shades of scarlet and crimson.

MIDWINTER SPLENDOUR: the bare branches of japonica carry clusters of beautiful blossom.

FEATURES

Also known as flowering quince, this multi-stemmed deciduous shrub grows from 2 to 3 m high with thorny stems. This long-lived shrub flowers early in its life and reaches maturity in 3–5 years. It is valued in the garden mostly for the blossom that appears on the bare branches in middle to late winter, rather than for the fruits that follow. There are many lovely cultivars available, with flowers in shades of scarlet, deep crimson, pink, white or apricot. Japonica may be grown as a specimen plant or as a background plant to smaller shrubs, bulbs and annuals.

CONDITIONS

Climate Not suited to the tropics or very warm areas. Best in areas with a cool to cold winter.

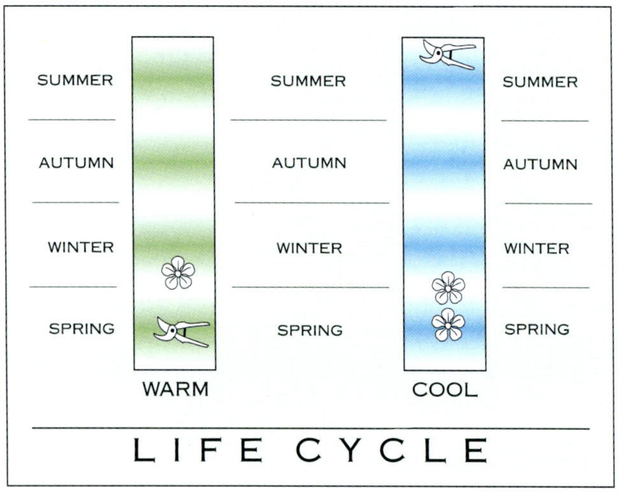

Aspect Must have at least half a day's sun but prefers full sun all day. This plant is tolerant of exposed, windy sites.

Soil Prefers well-drained soil but tolerates heavier soils better than many shrubs.

GROWING METHOD

Propagation Grow from semi-hardwood cuttings taken in late summer and autumn or from hardwood cuttings of dormant wood taken in winter.

Watering Regular watering is needed to establish but once plants are well established they are able to tolerate drought. They grow better, however, if they are given occasional deep waterings in hot, dry weather.

Fertilising Not essential but complete plant food may be applied in early spring as new growth starts.

Problems There are no particular pest or disease problems but fruits are susceptible to attack by Queensland fruit fly. It may be better to remove unripe fruits to avoid having to spray.

FLOWERING

Season From middle to late winter and continuing into early spring in cooler areas.

Fruit Flowers are followed by small, fragrant, quince-like fruits that ripen yellow if left on the bush. They are edible but are usually made into jams and preserves.

PRUNING

General Flowering branches can be cut for indoor decoration. Otherwise some of the older canes should be sawn out at ground level every year or two so as to make room for new growth. This should be done straight after flowering.

JUSTICIA

Justicia carnea

DELIGHTFULLY OLD-FASHIONED, the flowers of justicia come in both this lovely rose pink and a simple white. The pink is more traditional.

SUMMER-FLOWERING JUSTICIA is a good choice for a cottage-type garden in a warm climate. It likes shade.

FEATURES

Justicia was widely grown in earlier times for its decorative and long-lasting flowers. Flowers are usually 'old-rose' pink but there is a white form available too. An evergreen shrub with cane-like stems, it is long lived if old canes are cut out regularly. It reaches maturity, with a height of 1.5 m, in 2–3 years and is best used in mixed shrub plantings or to screen fences.

CONDITIONS

Climate Unsuitable for cold areas. Grows well in the tropics and other warm zones.

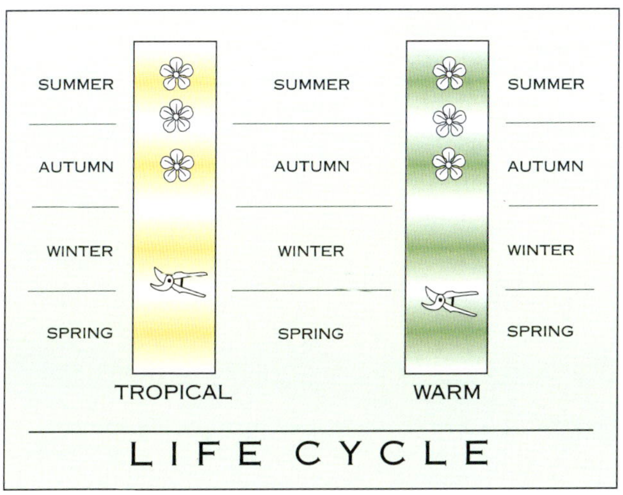

Aspect Needs shelter from strong wind. Prefers morning sun and afternoon shade, or a lightly shaded position.

Soil Needs well-drained soil with a high content of organic matter. Use well-decayed organic matter as a mulch.

GROWING METHOD

Propagation Tip cuttings can be taken through spring and summer. Plants can also be struck from semi-hardwood cuttings taken during autumn and early winter.

Watering Regular deep watering is needed to maintain the best looking growth and the most prolific and longest flowering.

Fertilising Apply complete plant food in early spring and again in midsummer.

Problems Not susceptible to any specific disease or insect attack but can be damaged by small snails that climb up to the top growth. Search for these and remove by hand.

FLOWERING

Season Long flowering period through summer and autumn months.

PRUNING

General Remove spent flowers as they fade. In late winter cut out canes that have already flowered at ground level so as to make room for new growth in spring.

KERRIA

Kerria japonica

A CHARMINGLY TANGLED MASS of bright yellow flowers in spring makes kerria, or Japanese rose, an attractive screening plant.

KERRIA FLOWERS can be single or double—this is the more common double version. The leaves colour attractively in autumn.

FEATURES

A deciduous shrub growing to about 2 m high with crowded, cane-like stems, kerria makes a good screening plant and can also be a feature of mixed shrub plantings. It is long lived if old canes are cut out regularly, but grows relatively slowly and takes over 5 years to reach maturity. Flowers appear from the first year. They are bright yellow and the serrated leaves colour yellow before falling in autumn. The form with double flowers, 'Plena', is commonly grown.

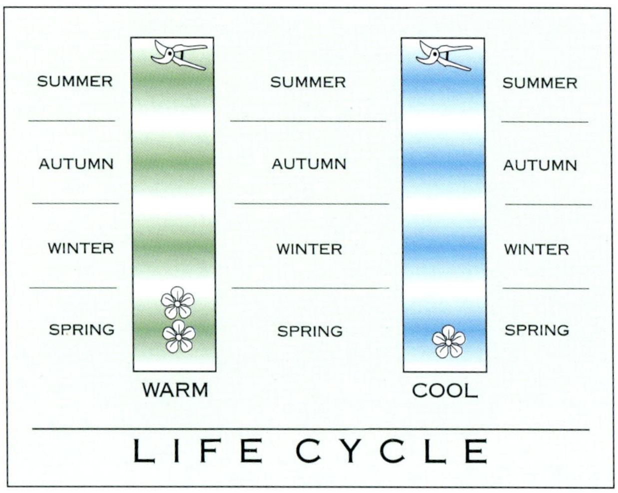

CONDITIONS

Climate Not suitable for the tropics; prefers a cool, moist climate.

Aspect Prefers full sun but tolerates shade for part of the day.

Soil Needs well-drained soil enriched with organic matter for best results, although it tolerates poorer soils as long as drainage is good.

GROWING METHOD

Propagation Strike from semi-hardwood cuttings taken in summer or early autumn. Old clumps can be divided into several plants.

Watering Tolerates drying out but gives best results if it is well watered regularly during the warmer months of the year.

Fertilising Apply complete plant food or blood and bone in late winter and again in midsummer.

Problems No particular pest or disease problems.

FLOWERING

Season The yellow flowers appear on the bush from early to late spring.

PRUNING

General Remove some of the older canes at ground level, after flowering has finished, to provide space for new growth.

LANTANA

***Lantana camara* cultivars**

COMPACT LANTANA SHRUBS are tough and drought resistant. In subtropical and tropical climates they can flower all year.

COMMON LANTANA is considered a noxious weed, but 'tame' varieties can look splendid cascading over a low wall or even in a pot.

FEATURES

Although the straight species, *L. camara,* is a declared noxious weed in many areas and has become a very troublesome invader of bushland, these dwarf cultivars can be considered 'safe' to grow as most are sterile or produce little seed. Dwarf forms rarely grow more than about 50 cm high and are ideal for planting in the foreground of mixed shrub borders. Some cultivars reach 2 m or so in height. The showy flowers may be red, yellow, orange, cream or white. These shrubs are not long lived, but they reach maturity in about 2 years. They flower from the first year.

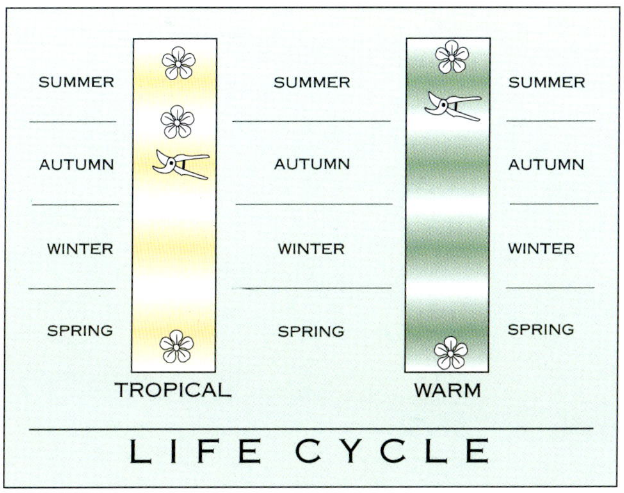

CONDITIONS

Climate Not suitable for cold areas. Needs a warm frost-free climate.

Aspect Needs full sun all day for the best growth and good flowering.

Soil Tolerates poor soil as long as it is well drained but much better growth will be made if the soil is enriched with organic matter.

GROWING METHOD

Propagation Tip cuttings can be taken all year round except during winter.

Watering Needs regular water to establish but once established tolerates quite dry conditions. Occasional deep waterings in dry weather produce better plants.

Fertilising Fertilising is not essential but complete plant food may be applied in late winter.

Problems No known pest or disease problems.

FLOWERING

Season From the middle of spring throughout the summer months.

PRUNING

General Prune while young to create a rounded, compact shape. Tip prune immediately after flowering—this should prevent any seed, which occasionally occurs in these forms, from setting and being spread.

Lasiandra

Tibouchina species and cultivars

THE GLORIOUS FLOWERS of the lasiandra give a wonderful splash of autumn colour. Flowers are usually purple, but this pink hybrid is lovely too.

LASIANDRA can be enjoyed in any warm-climate garden: it ranges in size from container-sized dwarf shrubs to small trees.

FEATURES

Also known as glory bush, lasiandras, with their rich purple flowers, are a spectacular feature of the late summer and autumn garden, and there are now many species and cultivars to grow. Long lived, they reach maturity in 5–10 years but flower from early in their lives. Lasiandras range in size from the dwarf form 'Jules', which grows about 75 cm high, to the popular 'Alstonville' of 3 to 4 m. Some of the species, such as *T. granulosa*, may grow into tree-like proportions. There are also some hybrids with pink or white flowers but the purple varieties remain the most popular with gardeners. 'Jules' makes a good container plant but the other varieties may be grown as specimens or as background plantings in mixed borders. They are native to central and south America.

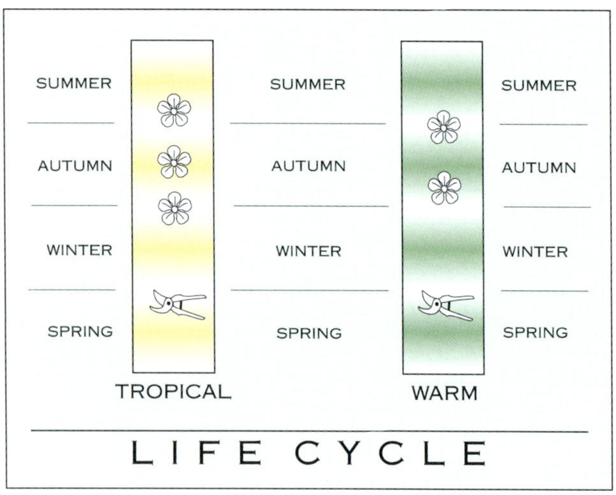

CONDITIONS

Climate Not suitable for cold areas; prefers a warm to hot climate.

Aspect Best in full sun all day with shelter from strong, cold wind.

Soil Must have well-drained soil with a high content of organic matter. Incorporate well-decayed manure or compost into the soil well ahead of planting time. Use organic material for mulching.

GROWING METHOD

Propagation Tip cuttings can be taken through spring, summer and autumn. It is essential to maintain high humidity around cuttings until they are well rooted.

Watering Regular deep watering is needed throughout the warmer months. Insufficient water results in small leaves and small, poor flowers.

Fertilising Complete plant food should be applied in early spring and again in midsummer.

Problems No particular pest or disease problems.

FLOWERING

Season Depends on variety chosen but most flower from late summer, and in some areas through autumn and into early winter. They can be a great feature of the garden in autumn.

PRUNING

General Tip prune in very early spring to keep growth compact. Don't prune in cold weather even if there is some winter damage as the damaged growth is giving some protection to the stems below it.

Lavender

Lavandula

THIS IS FRENCH LAVENDER but there can be some confusion over names. To make sure you get the plant you want, buy lavender in flower.

AROMATIC LAVENDER is essential in any cottage garden. Here Italian lavender is shown to advantage in terracotta pots.

FEATURES

Never out of fashion or favour, lavender forms a rounded shrub growing to 1 m or more high (dwarf forms are also available). The highly aromatic grey-green foliage is topped by spikes of lavender flowers, ranging from very pale to the deepest purple. Lavender reaches maturity in 3–5 years; it can be long lived in the right climate but may have a short life in areas with humid or wet summers. It can be grown with mixed shrubs, as a hedge or background to other plants, or in containers. Lavender is one of the essential components of the cottage garden. The common names of French, English or Italian lavender are applied to different species but even the experts find it hard to agree on which is which.

CONDITIONS

Climate Not suitable for the tropics or very warm, humid districts. The ideal climate has wet, cold winters and warm, dry summers.

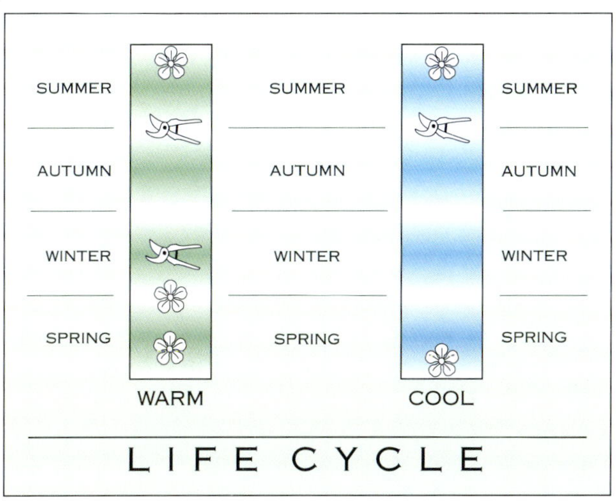

Aspect Needs an open situation in full sun with very good air circulation. Do not crowd it in with other plantings.

Soil Must have very well-drained and open soil. Coarse sandy or gravelly soil is ideal. Acid soils should be limed using 100 g per square metre.

GROWING METHOD

Propagation Tip cuttings of new growth that has firmed up can be taken from late spring through to autumn. Cuttings of side shoots with a heel of older wood can be taken during autumn and early winter.

Watering Needs regular water to establish but once established should not be overwatered. Tolerates long, dry spells without rain; give a very occasional deep soaking during the warmer months.

Fertilising Fertilising is not generally necessary. Pelletted poultry manure may be applied in early spring but the plant does quite well without it.

Problems No particular insect pests or disease known but plants rapidly succumb to root rot in heavy or overwet soils. In humid districts the foliage may die off inside or at the base of the plant. Remove dead growth and thin out foliage to improve air circulation.

FLOWERING

Season Varies with species. Many lavenders flower through late winter and spring but some species flower in summer.

Cutting Flowers are used fresh in posies or dried for a range of uses.

PRUNING

General Trim off spent flowers as they die. Tip pruning may be needed to keep growth compact. Overall shearing can be done in periods of rapid growth if a formal shape is wanted.

Lilac

Syringa vulgaris and *S.* x *hyacinthiflora* cultivars

FRAGRANT TRUSSES of lilac blossom are one of the great delights of spring in cool areas. They look beautiful, too.

COTTAGE GARDEN HIGHLIGHT: white lilac is here skilfully trained and pruned to form a romantic, sweetly scented canopy.

FEATURES

A great favourite for cool climate gardens, lilac has large trusses of sweetly perfumed flowers that may be white, pink, mauve, violet, crimson or shades in between. Flowers may be single or double and there is a great range of lovely cultivars. A deciduous shrub growing 2.5 to 3 m high, it may be grown as a specimen, as a screening plant or in massed plantings if the garden is large enough. Long lived, it matures in 5–10 years.

CONDITIONS

Climate Suitable only for cooler, moister areas, as most lilacs will not flower unless they get a good chilling during winter. If you live in a mild area, it may be worth seeking out the few varieties that flower in these areas.

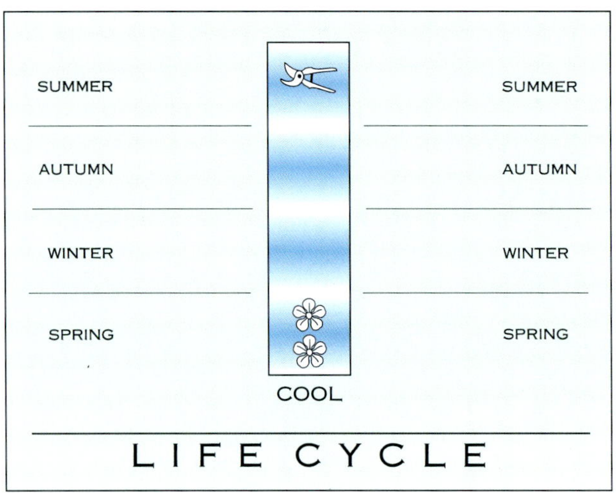

Aspect Needs full sun but protection from strong, drying winds.

Soil Needs well-drained soil that contains plenty of organic matter, which should be dug in well ahead of planting time. Mulch plants well with organic matter, too.

GROWING METHOD

Propagation Tip cuttings may be taken in late spring and summer but are not easy to root. Most lilac cultivars are budded or grafted onto privet rootstock, although more varieties are being grown on their own roots now. For an informed choice, select plants in flower at your nursery or consult books to see photographs of the named cultivars available.

Watering Lilacs should not be short of water during the warmer months and so deep, regular watering is essential. Commence deep watering when buds start to swell in spring.

Fertilising Apply complete plant food in early spring and in midsummer.

Problems No specific pest problems. Bacterial leaf spot is sometimes a problem for lilacs, especially in very wet seasons. Prune off the affected stems and, if it is necessary, spray the shrub with copper oxychloride.

FLOWERING

Season One of the delights of spring in cool areas.

Cutting Blossom can be cut for indoor decoration.

PRUNING

General Remove spent flower stems as soon as they fade. Suckering growth at the base of the plant can be cut out with a sharp spade.

LUCULIA

Luculia gratissima

LUCULIA CAN BE A CHALLENGE to grow, but take a bit of effort and you will be rewarded with large clusters of fragrant pink flowers that bloom through winter.

ORIGINALLY from the Himalayas, this evergreen shrub thrives in a warm climate.

FEATURES

This lovely evergreen shrub has pale pink, very fragrant flowers that appear during winter. It is a great asset to the garden if it performs well but it is difficult to grow and maintain. Plant it in a sheltered part of the garden as a specimen or among other shrubs. It is mostly seen about 3 m high but it can be taller and long lived in perfect conditions. It matures in 5–10 years and flowers from early in its life.

CONDITIONS

Climate Needs warm climate; unsuitable for cold zones. Does not tolerate frost, especially when young.

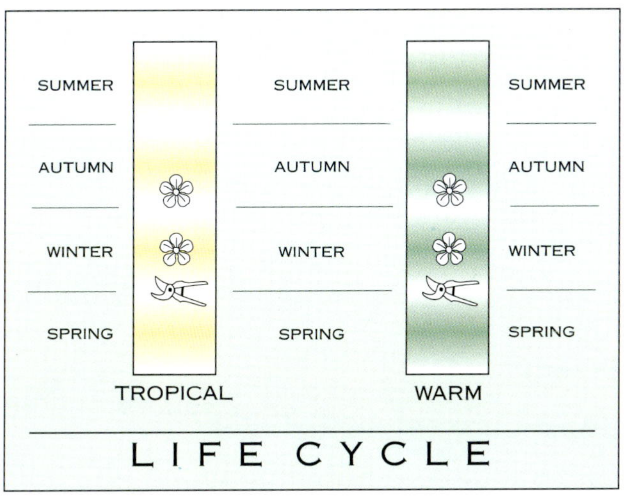

Aspect Must have shelter from strong wind and sun for at least half a day. Dappled sunlight all day is satisfactory but in these conditions growth may be somewhat sparse.

Soil Needs open, well-drained soil. Dig in rotted compost or manure well ahead of planting time. Luculia needs a cool root run and so should be mulched well. Make quite sure that the mulch is not packed up close to the stem.

GROWING METHOD

Propagation Tip cuttings can be taken during late spring and summer.

Watering Needs regular deep watering during warm months but soils should never be soggy.

Fertilising Apply blood and bone in early spring. Organic mulches such as cow manure or compost will also supply some nutrients.

Problems No specific pest or disease problems but plants have the unfortunate habit of dying for no apparent reason. It is probably related to the root conditions and so it is essential to maintain perfectly drained soil and have a cool root run.

FLOWERING

Season From the middle of autumn through until the middle of winter.

PRUNING

General Prune lightly at the end of winter after the flowers have faded.

Mahonia

Mahonia

SPIKY, HOLLY-LIKE LEAVES shield sprays of bright yellow flowers in winter or spring. They are followed by masses of decorative blue berries in autumn.

EASY TO GROW, Mahonia lomariifolia *makes an excellent talking point in the garden.*

FEATURES

These evergreen shrubs have shiny, spiky, holly-like leaves and multi-stemmed, cane-like growth. All mahonias have bright yellow flowers, mainly in winter or spring, and continue their decorative effect with berries through autumn into early winter. The blue berried forms are most popular as the colour is more unusual. Growing 1 to 3 m or so high, depending on species, they are good screening and background plants. Mahonias are long-lived shrubs reaching maturity after 5 years or more. Flowers and berries should be produced after 2 or 3 years.

CONDITIONS

Climate Best suited to cool, moist climates, they do not grow in the tropics or very warm zones.

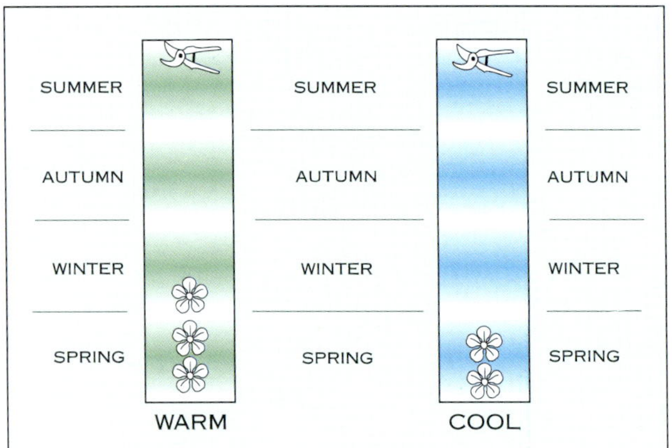

LIFE CYCLE

Aspect Mahonias prefer dappled sunlight or light shade. They also do quite well with morning sun but they must be shaded from hot afternoon sun.

Soil Need well-drained soil that is preferably high in organic matter. Mulching helps keep roots cool through summer.

GROWING METHOD

Propagation Can be grown from seed removed from the ripe berries. Semi-hardwood to hardwood cuttings may be taken in autumn or early winter.

Watering Water deeply and regularly during the warm months of the year. If the plant is growing where there is root competition from large trees, take special care to ensure that roots do not dry out.

Fertilising Apply blood and bone or complete plant food in early spring.

Problems Mahonia can provide an alternate host for the disease wheat rust although the species *M. aquifolium* and *M. bealei* have some resistance to this disease. Susceptible species should not be grown in rural areas where wheat is grown.

FLOWERING

Season Time depends on species chosen. The flowers are produced either through winter or spring.

Berries Berries follow the flowers. Some forms have red ones, others blue.

PRUNING

General Cut out thin, weak growth at ground level after flowering; otherwise no pruning is needed other than for shaping the clump.

May

Spiraea cantoniensis

DOUBLE-FLOWERED FORMS of may are the most popular but the single flowers have their own delights: they are more strongly perfumed.

ABUNDANT CLUSTERS of pure white flowers completely cover the arching branches of may in spring.

FEATURES

The name 'may', given to *Crataegus* species in England and Europe, is usually applied to this *Spiraea* in Australia. A deciduous shrub with graceful arching canes growing 2–3 m high, it can be used as a screening plant, in a mixed shrubbery or as a lawn specimen. Long lived, it takes at least 5 years to mature. Pure white single or double flowers are a feature in spring.

CONDITIONS

Climate Not suitable for the tropics; prefers a cool, moist climate.

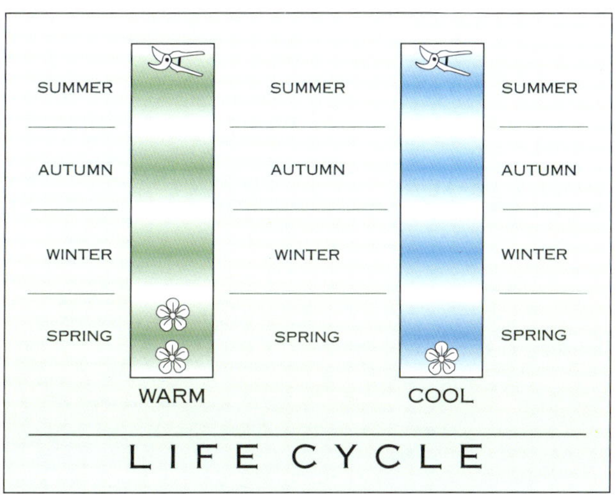

Aspect Needs full sun for compact growth and excellent flowering.

Soil Tolerates a wide range of soils but does best when planted in well-drained soil with added organic matter.

GROWING METHOD

Propagation May be struck from semi-hardwood cuttings taken in summer or early autumn, or from hardwood cuttings of dormant wood taken during winter.

Watering Needs regular watering to establish but once the plant is established it tolerates dry periods quite well. However, best results come from plants that are watered deeply during the warmer months.

Fertilising Apply complete plant food after flowering finishes in spring.

Problems No particular insect pest or disease problems.

FLOWERING

Season The white flowers are produced abundantly during spring.

PRUNING

General It is important not to spoil the natural arching growth habit of this plant. As flowers fade, stems should be tip pruned only. Some of the thicker, old canes can be cut out after flowering at ground level to create space for new young growth.

Mexican Orange Blossom

Choisya ternata

THE DELICIOUS SCENT of Mexican orange blossom fills the warm spring air around this lovely shrub.

WHITE FLOWERING Mexican orange blossom is here planted in perfect harmony with a pink flowering cherry.

FEATURES

An evergreen shrub with glossy leaves and scented white flowers, Mexican orange blossom grows 1.5–2 m tall. Suitable for mass planting as an informal hedge or in mixed shrub borders, it could also be grown in a large container. It takes about 5 years to reach its mature size, flowering from early in its life.

CONDITIONS

Climate Best suited to warmer climates, it tolerates colder areas if it is planted against a sheltered fence or wall.

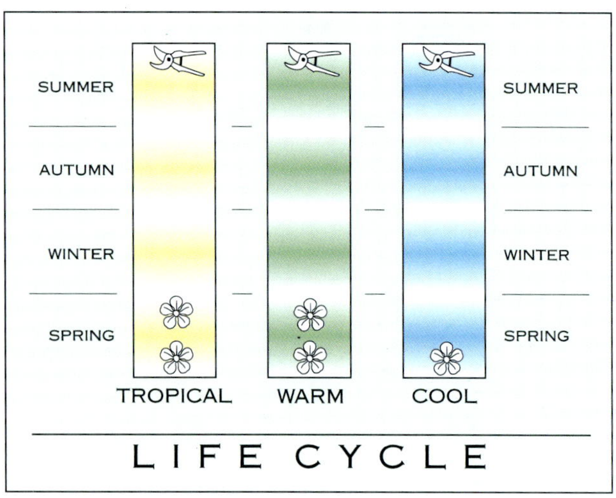

Aspect Needs warmth and shelter from strong, cold wind. Does best where it gets sun for all or most of the day.

Soil Needs well-drained soil that has been enriched with organic matter. Mulching with some well-decayed organic matter should improve the growth.

GROWING METHOD

Propagation Semi-hardwood cuttings can be taken in autumn and early winter.

Watering Needs regular deep watering during the warmer months.

Fertilising Apply complete plant food or blood and bone in early spring and again in midsummer.

Problems No specific pest or disease problems.

FLOWERING

Season The perfumed white flowers are produced during spring.

PRUNING

General Little pruning is needed beyond removal of the spent flower stems.

HINT

Shaping Although pruning is not usually necessary, Mexican orange blossom does respond well to clipping and some growers prefer to keep it trimmed to a formal shape.

Mint Bush

Prostanthera

THERE ARE MANY SPECIES of Prostanthera *but all have refreshingly mint-scented leaves. Most have purple flowers.*

PURPLE MINT BUSH is covered in a mass of mauve-purple flowers in spring.

FEATURES

Many species of this shrub are grown for their highly aromatic foliage and pretty blue-mauve flowers. These shrubs may grow 1–3 m or more tall, depending on the species. Plant them close to paths or the edges of gardens so that the fragrant foliage can be enjoyed. Of the 60 or more species, there is one suitable for almost all climates. Some species are quite short lived, most reaching maturity in 2–3 years and flowering even earlier.

CONDITIONS

Climate Not suitable for arid areas or the tropics. Local plant nurseries will probably stock those best suited to your area.

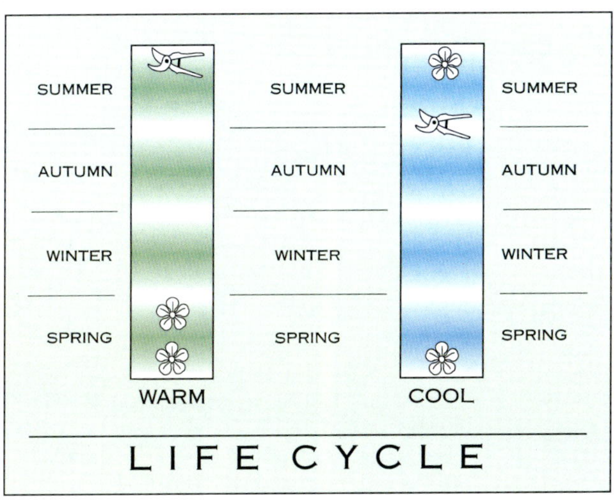

Aspect Generally prefers a site sheltered from strong wind with dappled sunlight or morning sun and afternoon shade.

Soil Soil should be well drained but have a high organic content. Roots must be kept cool in hot weather and so plants should be mulched. Pebbles or stones can be used as mulch to ensure that there is no build-up of humidity around stems.

GROWING METHOD

Propagation May be grown from seed but can also be grown from cuttings taken during late summer and early autumn.

Watering Must be watered regularly and deeply during hot, dry weather.

Fertilising May be grown without supplementary fertiliser but slow release granules or a little blood and bone could be applied in early spring.

Problems Root rot is the most common problem for mint bush and this is associated with poorly drained or overwet soils. Mint bushes grafted onto understocks of coast rosemary are more resistant to this problem.

FLOWERING

Season Time of flowering will depend on species but most mint bushes flower in spring, some continuing into summer.

PRUNING

General Cut back lightly after flowering to maintain dense growth habit but do not cut into the older, heavier wood.

Misty Plume Bush

Tetradenia riparia, syn. *Iboza riparia*

GRACEFUL SPRAYS of delicately tinted mauve-pink flowers make the misty plume bush an asset in the winter garden.

PHOTOGRAPHS cannot convey the delicious scent that is released from every part of the misty plume bush.

FEATURES

A semi-deciduous shrub growing 2 m or more high, the misty plume bush is valued for its graceful plumes of mauve-pink winter flowers and aromatic foliage. This long-lived shrub takes at least 5 years to reach maturity, but usually flowers within 2 years. It can be grown alone or in mixed shrub borders.

CONDITIONS

Climate Not suitable for cold areas, it is at its best in the warmest districts.

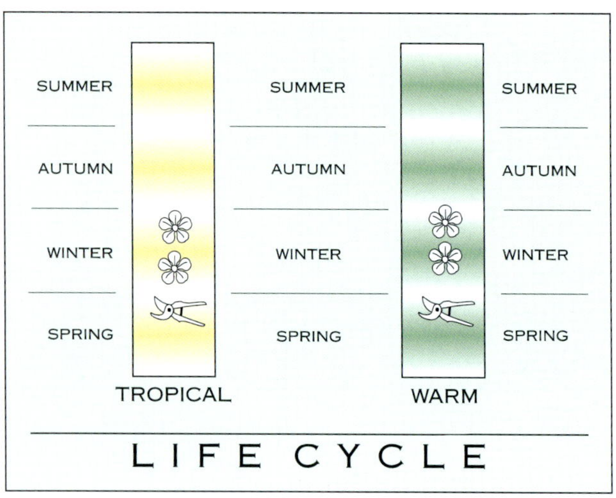

Aspect Needs a warm, sheltered position, preferably in full sun.

Soil Not fussy about soil type but the soil must be well drained. Tolerates all but the heaviest of clay soils.

GROWING METHOD

Propagation Take tip cuttings of new growth in spring.

Watering Tolerates long, dry periods better than many shrubs but benefits from deep watering every week or two during the warm months.

Fertilising Complete plant food or blood and bone may be applied in early spring but this is not essential.

Problems No particular pest or disease problems.

FLOWERING

Season From early winter to the middle of winter.

PRUNING

General Cut back immediately after flowering in winter. At least two-thirds of the previous year's growth can be removed.

HINT

Uses Like all plants with highly aromatic foliage, this shrub is best planted where it can be brushed as you pass. Widely planted by earlier generations, it should be used more often for its winter flowers and velvety foliage.

Morning, Noon & Night

Brunfelsia australis

PRETTY, OLD-FASHIONED FLOWERS open purple and then fade through mauve to white, all three colours appearing at the same time.

THE LOVELY SCENT of morning, noon and night drifts teasingly through the windows on warm spring evenings.

FEATURES

Also known as yesterday, today and tomorrow, *B. australis* may be sold as *B. bonodora*. The flowers open a deep violet colour and then fade to mauve and finally white, giving rise to the common names. All three colours appearing on the shrub give a lovely effect. The flowers also have a sweet scent, which is enhanced in the evening. Growing about 2–3 m high, this shrub is evergreen but may drop its leaves briefly in winter. In the right conditions it can be long lived, taking about 5 years to reach maturity but flowering from early in its life. It can be grown alone or in mixed shrub borders.

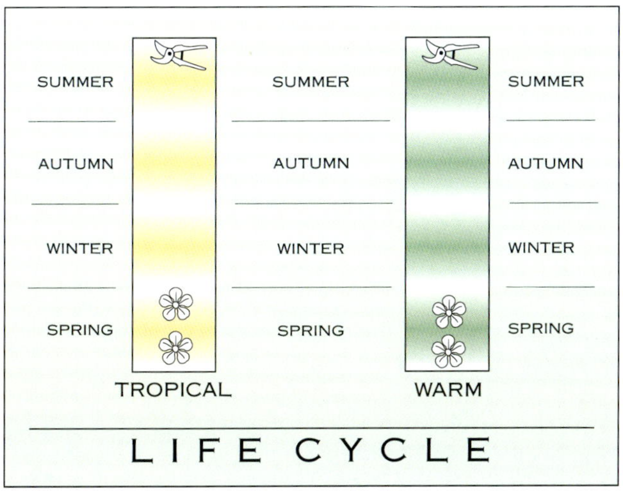

CONDITIONS

Climate Sensitive to cold and so best in warmer areas.

Aspect Prefers full sun but grows quite well with half a day's sun exposure.

Soil Needs well-drained soil and benefits from mulching to maintain soil moisture during hot weather.

GROWING METHOD

Propagation Can be grown from seed or from firm tip cuttings taken from late spring until autumn.

Watering Needs a good deep soaking about once a week in the warmer months.

Fertilising Fertilise with complete plant food, blood and bone or pelletted poultry manure in late winter or early spring.

Problems No particular pest or disease problems.

FLOWERING

Season Flowering period is spring.

PRUNING

General Little pruning is necessary but if shaping is needed, prune the bush immediately after the flowering period.

HINT

Position Site near the house where the perfume of its flowers can be enjoyed throughout spring.

Oleander

Nerium oleander

POPULAR OLEANDER has a long flowering period, and comes in a range of colours, including white, pink, apricot and crimson.

A DENSE SCREEN PLANTING of white oleander flatters a boring wooden fence and effectively gives privacy to this garden.

FEATURES

This hardy, evergreen shrub grows from 2 to 4 m high depending on the variety chosen, while there are some dwarf forms that grow to less than 1 m high. Oleanders are very useful for screening and windbreaks as they tolerate not only strong wind but salt-laden winds also. Oleanders are long lived and mature within 3–5 years. They flower from early in their life. These shrubs have a long flowering period and a good range of colour from which to choose: white, pink, cerise, crimson and apricot, in both single and double types. There is also a form popular with flower arrangers that has variegated cream and green leaves. One drawback with oleanders is that all parts of the plant are poisonous if eaten, and so take care if children are in the garden. The wood should not be used to fuel barbecues, either, as the smoke can permeate the food.

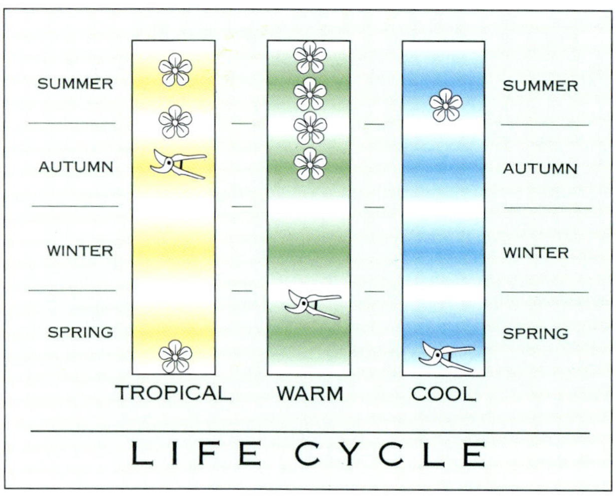

CONDITIONS

Climate Not suitable for very cold regions, oleander is best in warm climates but tolerates some frost. It is successfully grown in arid areas where water is available.

Aspect Needs full sun for best growth and flowering. Tolerates windy sites.

Soil Tolerates most soil types but not heavy, waterlogged soil. Does best in lighter soils with good drainage.

GROWING METHOD

Propagation Should strike easily from semi-hardwood cuttings taken in early autumn.

Watering Although oleander tolerates long, dry periods, the best results come from shrubs that are given occasional heavy waterings when weather is hot and dry.

Fertilising Fertilising is not essential. Complete plant food may be applied in early spring if soil is very poor and sandy.

Problems Plants are sometimes attacked by scale insects, which should be sprayed with white oil. There is a bacterial gall that produces lumps on the stems, flowers and pods. Prune off affected growth as soon as it is noticed. Disinfect secateurs between cuts.

FLOWERING

Season Usually in flower from late spring throughout summer and sometimes into autumn.

PRUNING

General Tip prune in spring; in the tropics they are best pruned after flowering. Cut back straggly bushes severely in late winter to restore shape.

ORANGE BROWALLIA

Streptosolen jamesonii

THE CLUSTERS of small, richly coloured yellow-orange-red flowers give orange browallia its nickname of marmalade bush.

THE WARMER the climate the better this cheerful, sun-loving shrub will flower. Here it is trained against a fence and lattice.

FEATURES

The long flowering display of yellow-orange-red flowers characteristic of orange browallia has given rise to another common name, marmalade bush. The multi-stemmed evergreen shrub grows to about 2 m high. It reaches maturity in 2–3 years and has a reasonable life span if old canes are cut out regularly. Flowers appear from early in the life of the plant. Orange browallia can be grown against a sunny fence, in mixed shrubberies or as a background to annuals. Its strong colours have considerable impact. The nectar in the flowers is attractive to some honey-eating birds. There is a smaller growing form, 'Ginger Meggs', which is sometimes available.

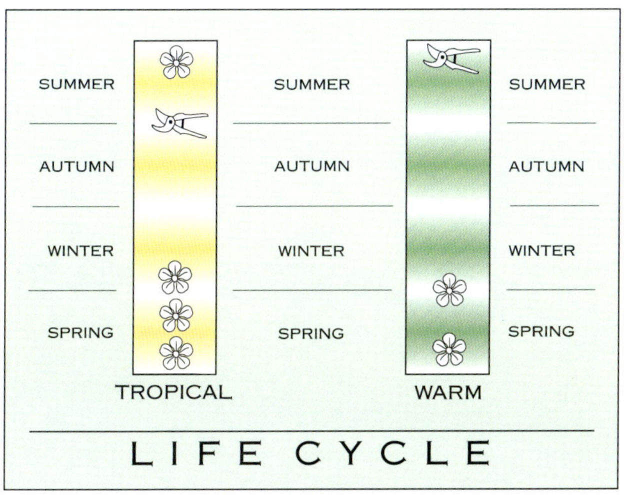

CONDITIONS

Climate Must have a warm, frost-free climate. The warmer the climate, the more vigorous and free flowering the plant is.

Aspect Must have full sun; needs some protection from wind.

Soil Needs well-drained soil. Most lighter soils are suitable and the addition of compost or manure to the soil prior to planting will improve results.

GROWING METHOD

Propagation Can be grown readily from tip cuttings taken in late spring and early summer or from semi-hardwood cuttings taken in late summer to early autumn.

Watering Needs regular deep watering during the warmer months. Mulching is beneficial as it helps conserve moisture.

Fertilising Apply complete plant food, blood and bone or poultry manure in late winter and midsummer.

Problems No particular insect pests or diseases.

FLOWERING

Season Main flowering period is late winter until late spring. There may be flowers intermittently through summer and autumn too.

PRUNING

General Cut back after the main flowering flush. Older canes can be cut out at ground level to make way for new growth.

ORANGE JESSAMINE

Murraya paniculata

SPRAYS OF FRAGRANT WHITE FLOWERS appear mainly in spring or early summer but can burst into bloom at any time after heavy rain.

AN ATTRACTIVE screening shrub, orange jessamine will grow as high as a house but can be kept smaller by pruning.

FEATURES

This evergreen shrub has attractive, glossy foliage and white, very fragrant flowers. It grows at least 3 m high and 2 m or more wide. Long lived, it takes about 10 years to maturity but flowers from early in its life. An excellent screening shrub or background planting, it is often grown as an informal hedge. It can also be grown in a container for some years.

CONDITIONS

Climate Needs a warm, frost-free climate. Not suitable for cool zones.

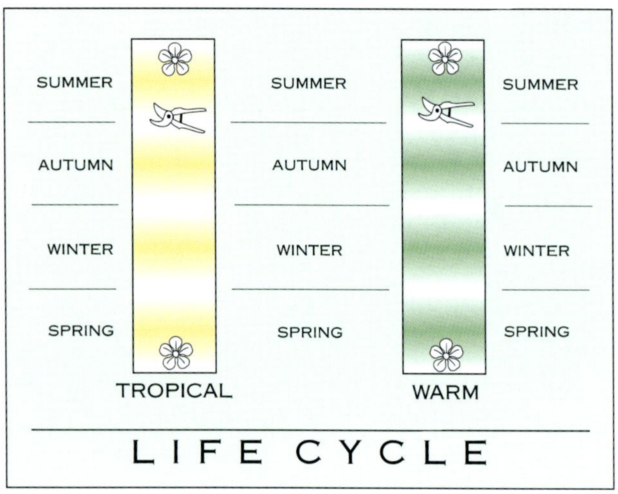

Aspect In the tropics almost any situation will do but elsewhere it should be grown in full sun, preferably with some shelter given from the coldest winds.

Soil Needs well-drained soil enriched with organic matter that has been dug in well ahead of planting time. Mulching with organic material also helps to provide good growing conditions for this plant.

GROWING METHOD

Propagation Can be grown from semi-hardwood cuttings taken in late summer and early autumn. Where berries are set and ripened, it can be grown from seed that has been removed from its fleshy covering.

Watering Needs regular deep watering during dry periods in the warmer months.

Fertilising Apply complete plant food in early spring and again in midsummer.

Problems No particular insect pest or disease problems.

FLOWERING

Season The main flowering period is late spring or early summer but orange jessamine has a habit of bursting into bloom at other times, especially after heavy rain.

PRUNING

General Can be tip pruned at any time after flowering to maintain dense growth.

PENTAS

Pentas lanceolata

PENTAS IS VALUED by gardeners for its very long and abundant flowering period over spring, summer and autumn.

CHARMING PENTAS adds welcome colour to a shady spot in this warm-climate cottage garden. It is very sensitive to frost.

FEATURES

A great addition to the warm climate garden, pentas has a very long flowering period. The flowers come in a wide colour range that includes white, palest pink, lavender, cerise, crimson and bicoloured cerise and white. The soft shrubby plant grows to about 1 m high, reaching maturity in 2–3 years. With regular pruning it may live for about 10 years but new plants should be started after about 5 years. It can be planted *en masse* or with other plants.

CONDITIONS

Climate Needs a warm, frost-free climate. Pentas turns black at the slightest sign of frost.

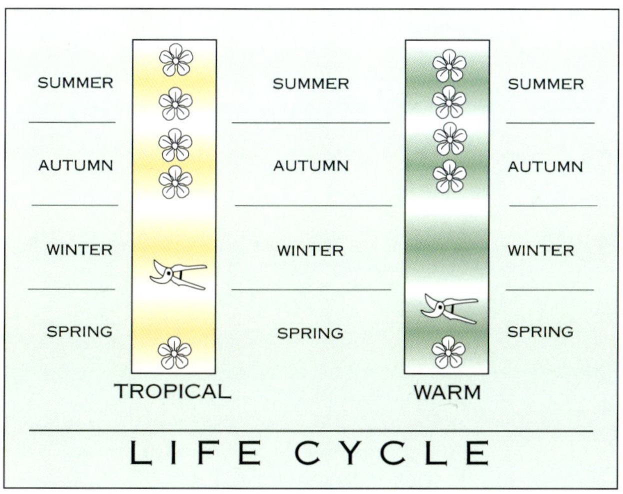

Aspect Needs at least half a day's sun for best results with shelter from strong wind.

Soil Needs well-drained soil, preferably enriched with organic matter. Mulch plants with well-rotted organic matter too.

GROWING METHOD

Propagation Can be grown easily from cuttings taken throughout spring and summer, and until early autumn.

Watering Needs regular deep watering throughout the warmer months in dry weather.

Fertilising Don't overdo the fertiliser or you will have lots of soft, sappy growth at the expense of flowers. Apply complete plant food in early spring and again in midsummer.

Problems No particular insect pest or disease problems.

FLOWERING

Season The long flowering period starts in late spring and continues until early winter.

PRUNING

General Cut back stems that have flowered in late winter or early spring. Tip prune to remove spent flower heads during summer and autumn. Cutting for the vase is one way of doing this.

HINT

Pentas can be grown in a container if desired. Flowers can be cut for posies, too.

PHOTINIA

Photinia species and cultivars

GENEROUS CLUSTERS of tiny white flowers appear in spring, to be followed by a flush of bright red berries.

ONE OF THE FINEST of all hedging plants, photinia is valued for its brilliant red young leaves that turn dark green with maturity.

FEATURES

These evergreen shrubs, most often used as hedges and screens, are valued for the bright pinky-red new growth that appears with every growth flush. The flowers are clusters of very small white blooms that appear profusely on the bushes in spring. Heights of the shrubs vary somewhat with species but, unpruned, most reach between 4 and 5 m. These shrubs are long lived and take about 10 years to mature, although flowers appear from early in their life. However, many gardeners never allow their photinias to flower but prune as soon as buds appear to increase the young leaf growth. The foliage is the main reason for growing this shrub.

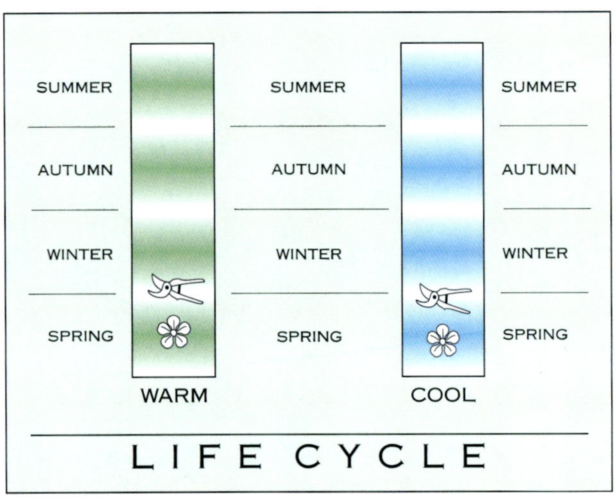

CONDITIONS

Climate *P. glabra* 'Rubens' and *P. serratifolia* are best suited to cool, moist climates. *P.* x *fraseri* 'Robusta' prefers a warm to cool district.

Aspect Prefers full sun. It grows in partly shaded situations but is not as dense there and does not produce such bright new growth.

Soil Must have well-drained soil. Photinia does not tolerate heavy, waterlogged soils.

GROWING METHOD

Propagation Semi-hardwood cuttings taken in autumn or early winter should strike well.

Watering Needs regular deep watering during the warmer months of the year.

Fertilising Apply complete plant food in late winter or early spring.

Problems Scale insects may be a problem from time to time: they should be sprayed with white oil. Photinias are very susceptible to root rot in heavy, poorly drained soils.

FLOWERING

Season Flowering period is spring. Commencement and duration varies with species.

PRUNING

General Major pruning should be done in late winter. Many growers like to tip prune often throughout the growing season so that they obtain flushes of the new reddish growth over some months.

Pieris

Pieris japonica*, syn. *Andromeda japonica

YOUNG PIERIS LEAVES are an eye-catching shade of pink—as they mature they darken to green.

NOT ONLY BLESSED with attractive leaves, in winter and spring pieris also produces sprays of flowers that resemble lily-of-the-valley.

FEATURES

Pieris is a lovely evergreen shrub growing 2 or 3 m high and producing sprays of white or pink-tinged flowers in spring. The young foliage is pink or reddish and is a real feature of some of the named cultivars available. Pieris is probably best bought in spring so that you can be sure of obtaining the form you want. In the right climate pieris is long lived, maturing after about 5 years but flowering from early in its life. It can be grown in mixed shrub borders, as a specimen or in a container.

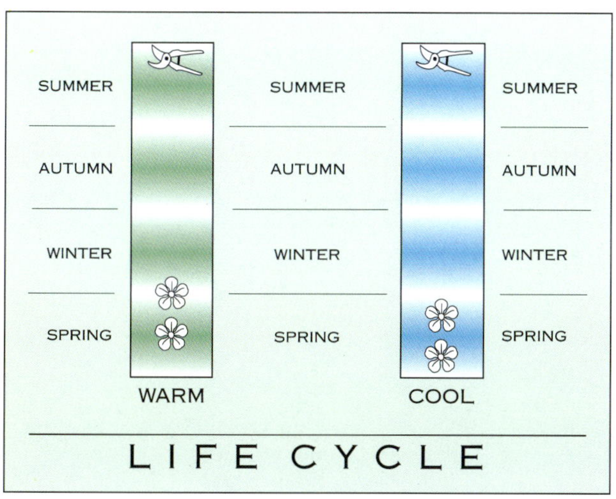

CONDITIONS

Climate Prefers a cool, moist climate and is not suitable for tropical or very warm districts.

Aspect Needs shelter from strong wind and hot afternoon sun. Pieris does best in dappled sunlight or where direct sunlight is restricted to mornings.

Soil Must have well-drained soil. Dig in generous amounts of well-decayed organic material well ahead of planting time. Plants should also be mulched with organic matter.

GROWING METHOD

Propagation Best grown from semi-hardwood cuttings taken through summer to early autumn.

Watering Regular deep watering is essential during the warmer months of the year.

Fertilising Apply blood and bone or azalea and camellia food during late winter and then again in the middle of summer.

Problems No particular insect pest or disease problems.

FLOWERING

Season From late winter to the middle of spring.

PRUNING

General Tip prune to remove spent flowers as they fade. No other pruning is generally necessary.

Plumbago

Plumbago auriculata

CLUSTERS OF DELIGHTFUL SKY-BLUE FLOWERS cover plumbago from spring right through into autumn.

FAST-GROWING PLUMBAGO makes an excellent informal hedge but needs to be kept in shape by severe pruning after flowering.

FEATURES

Unpruned, this evergreen shrub is fairly loose and open in growth but it is generally pruned and shaped to promote bushy, compact growth. It reaches 2–3 m high and the pale sky-blue flowers are produced over a very long season, beginning early in the life of the plant. Plumbago is long lived if it is pruned regularly, maturing after 2–3 years. There is also a white-flowered form of plumbago that is not as vigorous in habit. Plumbago is often grown against fences and walls and can make a good hedge. It is a good shrub to plant near pools or summer entertaining areas because of its long flowering season.

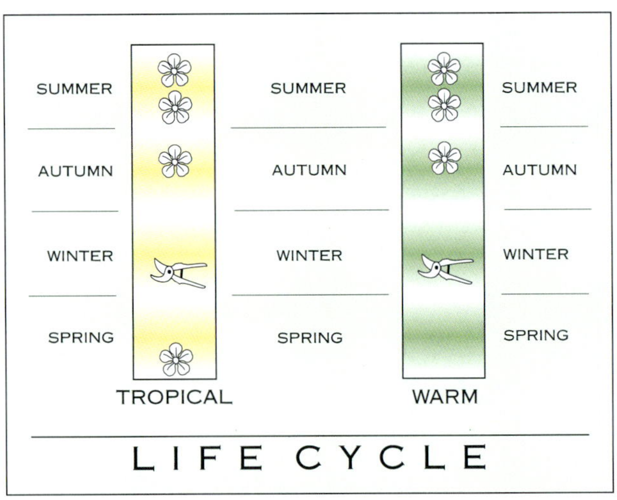

CONDITIONS

Climate Not suitable for cold areas. It performs best in warm to hot areas, including the tropics.

Aspect Prefers full sun all day but is fairly satisfactory with half a day's sun.

Soil Grows in most soil types but the drainage must be good.

GROWING METHOD

Propagation Tip cuttings can be taken from late spring through until early autumn.

Watering Needs regular watering to establish but once it is established it tolerates quite long dry periods. However, deep watering every week or two in hot, dry weather produces more attractive plants.

Fertilising Don't overdo it. Light feeding with any complete plant food in late winter to early spring is sufficient.

Problems No particular pest or disease problems affect this plant.

FLOWERING

Season From late spring throughout summer into autumn. Late summer usually sees the peak flowering performance.

PRUNING

General Needs hard cutting back in late winter. It can also be tip pruned or shaped at any time during the growing season.

Poinsettia

Euphorbia pulcherrima

THE LARGE, POINTED 'PETALS' of this cream poinsettia are really bracts supporting the tiny, insignificant central flowers.

THESE RED POINSETTIAS provide a spectacular midwinter display to cheer their owners and passers-by alike.

FEATURES

Evergreen in the tropics and deciduous in other areas, poinsettia is grown for its brilliant display of winter 'flowers' (in reality, bracts). Available with bright scarlet, crimson, pink, cream or white bracts, it normally grows 3–4 m high. A dwarf form is cultivated as a pot plant. Poinsettia is long lived if pruned regularly to cut out old canes. It matures in 3–5 years and flowers from early in its life.

CONDITIONS

Climate Best in the tropics and warm areas; not suitable for cold districts.

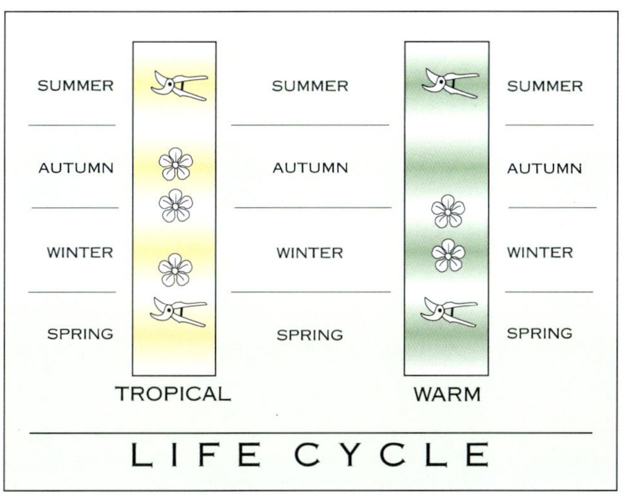

Aspect Needs shelter from strong wind. Poinsettia should be grown in full sun in the warmest part of the garden.

Soil Needs well-drained soil. Soils that are enriched with decayed organic matter will produce the best results.

GROWING METHOD

Propagation Can be grown from tip cuttings taken during the growing season but the easiest method is to pot up hardwood cuttings after pruning in late winter or very early spring.

Watering Once established, poinsettia tolerates long dry periods well. However, the best results come from plants that are watered deeply every week or two.

Fertilising Any all-purpose plant food can be applied in late winter and again in midsummer.

Problems No particular insect pest or disease problems.

FLOWERING

Season Flowering time varies according to the district but is somewhere between late autumn and late winter.

PRUNING

General Cut back hard after flowering, in late winter or very early spring. A second, lighter cutting in late summer should help produce more potential flowering growth. The milky sap is quite caustic, so wear gloves and protect your eyes while pruning.

POMEGRANATE

***Punica granatum* and cultivars**

BELL-SHAPED FLOWERS are an attractive feature of the pomegranate. They can be scarlet, as here, or pink or white.

POMEGRANATE is grown mainly for the delicious, decorative fruit that appears in late summer. Double-flowering forms do not produce fruit.

FEATURES

The pomegranate is a deciduous shrub growing 3–4 m high with bright scarlet flowers followed by orange-red fruit. Among the cultivars are forms with single or double flowers in cream, apricot or salmon. The double forms do not produce fruit. Most ornamental varieties are dwarf forms of the species. Pomegranates are long lived and take over 5 years to mature. The first flowers appear early in the life of the plant. Pomegranates can be grown as specimen plants, as an informal hedge or in mixed shrub borders. They are native to south-west Asia.

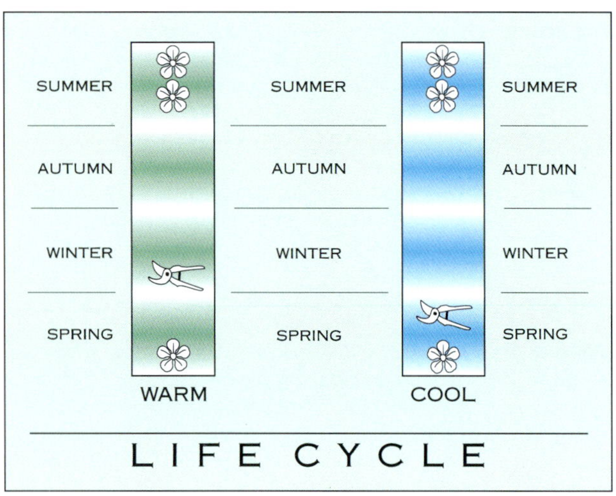

CONDITIONS

Climate Not suitable for the tropics but very hardy in most other climates. Pomegranate tolerates low temperatures as well as very high temperatures and low humidity, and so it is suitable for arid regions.

Aspect Needs full sun to achieve its best growth.

Soil Prefers an open, well-drained soil. Tolerates poor soils but better growth results if organic matter is added to the soil before planting.

GROWING METHOD

Propagation Can be grown from semi-hardwood cuttings taken in summer and early autumn or from hardwood cuttings of dormant wood taken during winter.

Watering Tolerant of dry conditions, it performs better if it is given occasional deep watering in hot, dry weather.

Fertilising Apply complete plant food in late winter.

Problems No particular insect pest or disease problems.

FLOWERING

Season From late spring throughout summer.

Fruit The decorative fruit appear from late summer until early winter. The fruit is edible.

PRUNING

General Prune to shape in late winter or early spring to maintain dense growth habit.

PORT WINE MAGNOLIA

Michelia figo

SMALL MAROON FLOWERS are hardly visible but they make their presence felt by a rich, heavy perfume that may even be overpowering.

PORT WINE MAGNOLIA makes a shapely, easy-care shrub or small tree for a corner of the garden.

FEATURES

An evergreen shrub with glossy green leaves, in spring the port wine magnolia has small maroon flowers that are heavily scented. It is a long-lived shrub, taking 5–10 years to mature although flowers will appear after approximately 3–5 years. Growing to about 3 m high, it is often used for screening, informal hedging or as a background to other plantings. The common name sometimes causes confusion between this shrub and the more tree-like *Magnolia* x *soulangiana*.

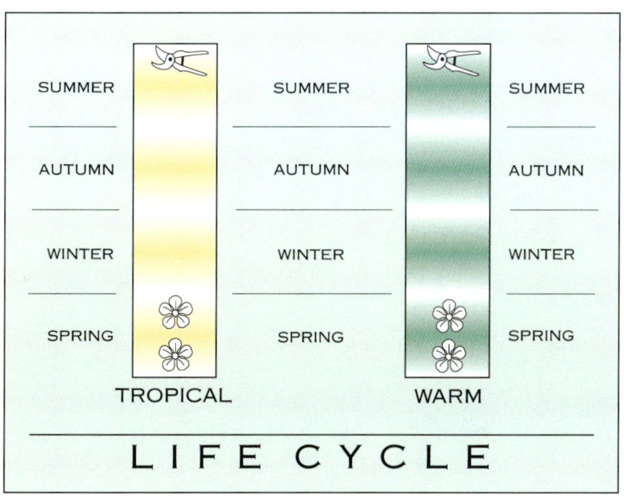

CONDITIONS

Climate Needs a warm climate that is frost-free.

Aspect Prefers a warm position sheltered from strong wind. Does not tolerate salt wind at all. Best in full sun.

Soil Needs well-drained soil that has been enriched with organic matter well ahead of planting time. Plants should be mulched with organic matter too.

GROWING METHOD

Propagation Strike from semi-hardwood cuttings taken in late summer or early autumn.

Watering Needs regular deep watering in dry weather during the warm months of the year.

Fertilising Apply blood and bone or azalea and camellia food in late winter and again in midsummer.

Problems Generally trouble-free but it can be attacked by a scale insect that is very damaging. As this is a hard scale it must be treated with an insecticide plus white oil.

FLOWERING

Season From early to late spring. The flowers are not showy but they do produce a lovely fragrance.

PRUNING

General Prune lightly after the flowers fade.

PRIDE OF MADEIRA

Echium fastuosum

TOWER OF JEWELS is another common name for these magnificent spikes of bright blue flowers.

GIVE PRIDE OF MADEIRA room to grow as it can spread to more than 2 m across, but it's an excellent plant for a sheltered seaside garden.

FEATURES

A somewhat sprawling shrub with grey-green leaves, pride of Madeira grows to about 1.5 m high and spreads to 2 m or more across. It has many tall spikes of brilliant blue flowers in spring. Long lived only in Mediterranean climates, it matures in 3–5 years and flowers from early in life. It is not a shrub for very small gardens and needs an open position.

CONDITIONS

Climate Not tolerant of heavy frost, but grows in cool districts in frost-free parts of the garden. Best in warm to hot areas.

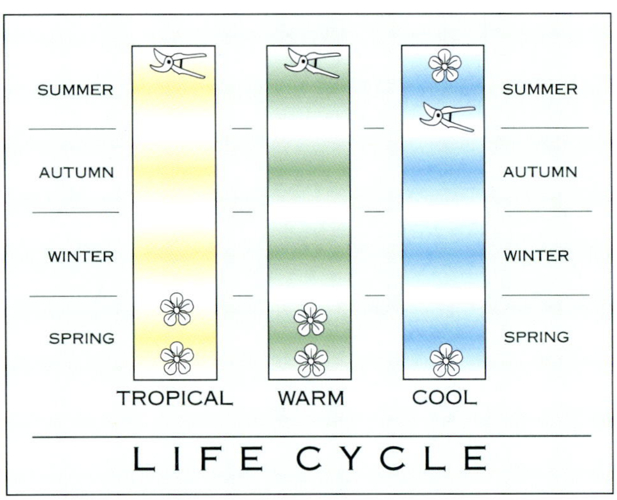

Aspect Needs full sun all day and must have very good air circulation.

Soil Must have very well-drained soil. Does best in quite poor, coarse, sandy or gravelly soils. Before planting, add lime or dolomite to soils known to be very acid. Apply about 100 g per square metre.

GROWING METHOD

Propagation Can be grown from seed. Try cuttings of side shoots taken from an older stem with a small heel of the older wood during summer and early autumn. They can, however, be difficult to root without glasshouse conditions and bottom heat.

Watering Tolerates very dry conditions and should need only a very occasional deep watering in prolonged dry weather.

Fertilising Probably best with no supplementary fertiliser at all.

Problems No particular pest or disease problems but this plant dies very quickly in poorly drained, heavy soils.

FLOWERING

Season From spring through to early summer.

PRUNING

General Cut back after flowering to remove spent flower heads. Trailing growth that is too vigorous can be cut back at any time during the growing season.

PRUNUS

Prunus x *blireana*

IN LATE WINTER AND SPRING the bare branches of prunus are covered in a lavish display of double pink blossoms.

PRUNUS BLOSSOMS need to be sheltered from the wind but they make a beautiful sight. Red-brown leaves follow in late spring.

FEATURES

A deciduous shrub or small tree 3–5 m high and with a neat, vase-shaped habit, prunus is suitable for small gardens or for avenue planting. It has abundant double pink flowers in late winter to early spring before the bronze-green leaves appear. Prunus are long lived, taking about 10 years to mature. They flower early but flowers increase with age.

CONDITIONS

Climate Not suitable for arid areas or the tropics; adapts to most climates and is very cold hardy.

Aspect Needs full sun for best performance. Ideally it should be sheltered from strong wind or the display of blossom will be ruined.

Soil Prefers a well-drained soil that has been enriched with organic matter. Mulching with organic matter is important in retaining soil moisture in warm, dry weather.

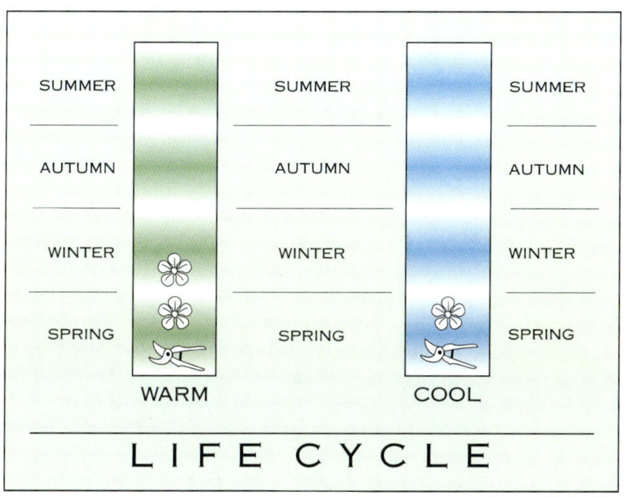

GROWING METHOD

Propagation Not easy for the home gardener to propagate as it is normally shield budded onto seedling understocks of other species of plums.

Watering Needs regular deep watering, especially when in bud and flower. Although fairly tolerant of dry periods, deep watering during dry weather is desirable.

Fertilising Apply complete plant food or blood and bone in spring after flowering finishes.

Problems No particular pest or disease problems.

FLOWERING

Season Late winter to early spring.

Cutting Stems of partially open blossom can be cut for the vase.

PRUNING

General Little pruning is needed as it tends to be self-shaping into its characteristic vase shape. However, it may be necessary to cut out lateral growths that crowd the centre of the shrub. This should be done in spring after flowering.

RHODODENDRON

Rhododendron

FEW SHRUBS CAN EQUAL RHODODENDRONS for a spectacular display of colour in late winter and early spring. This skilfully planned garden features a bold planting of white and pink rhododendrons framed by dark foliage that enhances rather than competes with the flowers.

FEATURES

Broad-leaf rhododendrons, with their spectacular show of large trusses of flowers in delicate pastels or strong vibrant colours, are the key feature of many lovely cool climate gardens. With the enormous range of varieties available they can be the mainstay of the garden for months from late winter until the end of spring. The Vireya rhododendrons, too, are always eye-catching when in bloom, the flowers set off by the perfection of the glossy foliage. They prefer a humid climate and their variable flowering habit leads to lovely surprises when they produce an unexpected flush of blooms. Rhododendrons are long lived and reach maturity in about 5–10 years. They will flower from their first year.

TYPES

Broad-leaf Broad-leaf rhododendrons are generally evergreen shrubs that range from less than 1 m to tree-like species with the greatest range around 3–4 m in height. Most have rather leathery leaves that are often somewhat hairy on the underside. Flowers are borne in large showy trusses in white, pink, red, blue, mauve, purple, cream, yellow or orange. Some are fragrant. There is an enormous range of species and cultivars available. Broad-leaf rhododendrons are cool climate plants. They may be grown as specimens but look spectacular when mass planted.

Vireya Rarely growing more than 2 m high, these evergreen shrubs have mid-green glossy leaves. Some are fairly open in habit, others more compact and densely foliaged. Flowering is variable and may be more than once a year. Colours range from white, yellow, apricot and salmon through to pinks and bright red. There are many cultivars, mostly in 'sunset' shades. Vireyas do well as understorey plants under tall trees but can be planted in a mixed shrub border. They are suitable for container growing and some varieties also do well in hanging baskets.

CONDITIONS

Climate Broad-leaf rhododendrons are suitable for cool to cold climates only, although there are a few varieties, for example 'Broughtonii' and 'Mrs E.C. Stirling', that will perform well in warmer zones. Vireyas need a frost-free, humid climate in the cool to warm zones. In arid areas or areas of low humidity they may be best grown in a shadehouse.

Aspect They need shelter from strong wind and prefer morning sun and afternoon shade or the light shade of tall trees.

Soil Need well-drained soil with a high organic content. Dig in copious quantities of well-decayed organic matter before planting and mulch well with organic matter. Vireyas are surface rooting plants: never plant them too deeply. Spread the roots, cover with soil and top with leaf litter, old manure or compost.

ABOVE: Ruffled petals of a broad-leaf rhododendron hybrid. BELOW: The Vireya 'Island Splendour'.

THE LOVELY TUBULAR FLOWERS of the Vireya rhododendron 'Peach Delight' will indeed delight any rhododendron fancier.

GROWING METHOD

Propagation Take semi-hardwood cuttings of the current season's growth through summer to early autumn. Hormone rooting powder increases the strike rate. Cuttings of broad-leafs can be slow to form roots; Vireyas strike more readily.

Watering Must be kept well watered during the warmer months and in dry, windy weather. Even in cool weather Vireyas should never be bone dry.

Fertilising For broad-leafs apply blood and bone or azalea and camellia food as blooming finishes in spring. A further light dressing may be applied in midsummer. Blood and bone or slow release granular fertilisers suit Vireyas best.

Problems Broad-leaf plants can be attacked by azalea lace bug, petal blight, fungal leaf spot and two-spotted mite but they are not as susceptible to these problems as azaleas. On Vireyas, azalea lace bug and thrips can be a problem, also powdery mildew in some areas. See the entry for azaleas for more detailed information.

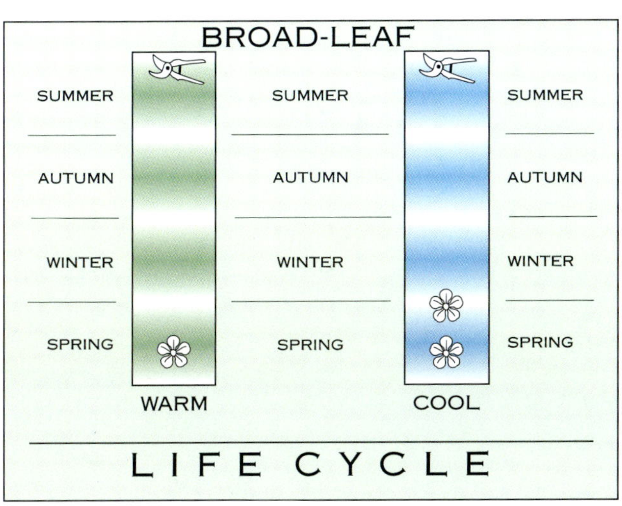

FLOWERING

Season Depending on the variety, broad-leaf rhododendrons may be in flower any time between late winter and late spring. In their habitats, Vireyas flower from late summer through to early winter but in cultivation flowering time is variable and plants may flower more than once a year.

PRUNING

General Little or no pruning is needed. If necessary, it should be done straight after flowering.

HINT

Buy locally If you live in a mild coastal district, it can be tempting to buy some glorious rhododendron you've seen in a cool climate garden, but think twice as you'll probably end up with a struggling plant of little ornamental value.

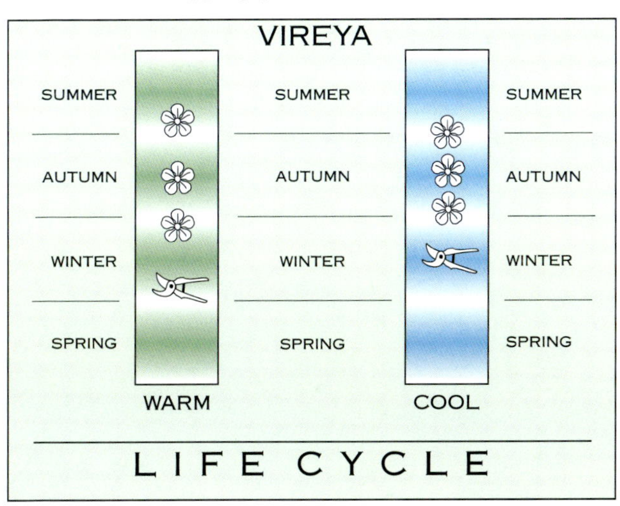

Rock Rose

Cistus

CHARMING FLOWERS that bloom right through summer are a feature of rock rose. This lilac one shows the characteristic red blotches.

AN AROMATIC SHRUB with rose-like flowers, the rock rose comes from the Mediterranean and is valued for its drought resistance.

FEATURES

These small evergreen shrubs, native to the Mediterranean regions, range in size from less than 1 m to 2 m or so tall. Flowers are not long lasting but are quite profuse—they come in white, pink, crimson or lilac with some varieties having five dark red blotches at the base of the petals. Plants mature in 3–5 years, depending on species, but begin to flower early in life. They make a fine informal hedge and smaller species can be grown in containers.

CONDITIONS

Climate The Mediterranean type of climate with hot, dry summers and cool, wet winters suits them best. They do poorly in areas with summer rainfall and where humidity is high.

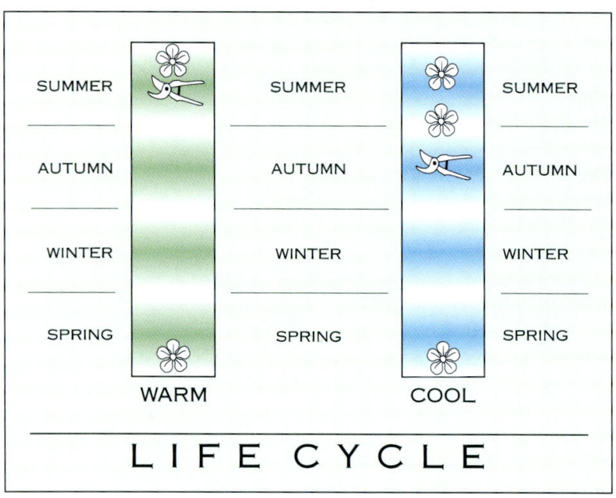

Aspect Must have full sun all day for best results. Rock rose tolerates strong wind, including salt-laden sea winds. It does remarkably well on exposed sites.

Soil Needs coarse sandy or gravelly soil that drains very quickly; does not tolerate heavy soils that remain wet for any length of time. Occurs naturally on well-drained limestone based soil. If your soil is acid, you should add lime, about 100 g per square metre, before planting.

GROWING METHOD

Propagation Species can be grown from seed or cuttings. Firm tip cuttings can be taken through summer until early autumn. Cultivars must be grown from cuttings.

Watering Needs regular water to establish, but once they are established these plants prefer to have only occasional deep waterings, and those only in very dry periods.

Fertilising Needs little or no fertiliser. A light dressing of complete plant food may be applied in very early spring.

Problems No particular pest or disease problems as long as growing conditions are suitable.

FLOWERING

Season Most species and cultivars flower from late spring through summer.

PRUNING

General Regular tip pruning is needed when plants are young so as to form a dense, compact bush. More mature plants should be cut back straight after they finish flowering.

RONDELETIA

Rondeletia amoena

SWEETLY SCENTED, the soft pink flowers of rondeletia appear in spring. They are excellent for cutting to take indoors.

PINK ON PINK—graceful clusters of rondeletia flowers look very effective against the background of a harmonising wall.

FEATURES

This dense evergreen shrub is multi-stemmed and grows to about 3 m high. It is native to southern Mexico and Panama. Long lived, it takes 5–10 years to mature but begins to flower early in its life. The clusters of pale pink, scented flowers are borne profusely from late winter until the middle of spring. It is a good shrub for screening or background planting but can also be grown as a specimen. Growth should be dense if grown in full sun but it thins out in sites that are heavily shaded.

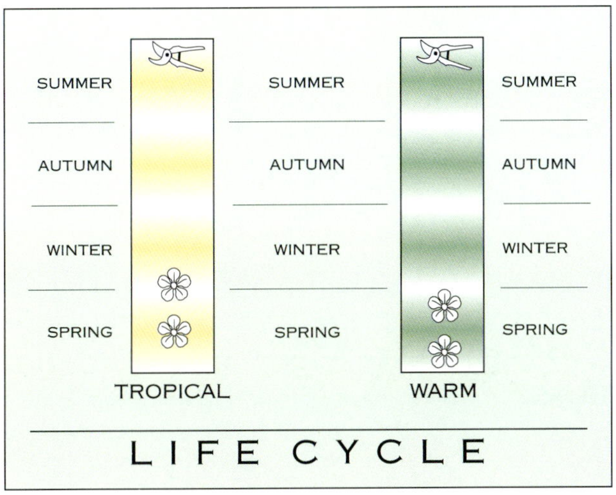

CONDITIONS

Climate Needs a warm, frost-free climate.

Aspect Needs a warm position in full sun with shelter from strong or cold wind.

Soil Needs well-drained soil with plenty of compost or manure added well ahead of planting time. Organic mulches should be used too.

GROWING METHOD

Propagation Grows from semi-hardwood cuttings taken in late spring or very early summer.

Watering Needs regular deep watering throughout the warmer months with only the very occasional watering in a dry winter.

Fertilising Apply blood and bone or complete plant food in late winter and again in midsummer.

Problems No particular insect pest or disease problems.

FLOWERING

Season From late winter through to the middle of spring or longer.

PRUNING

General Prune after flowering to help maintain the compact, dense habit. Very old shrubs may need to have some of the oldest woody canes removed at ground level.

Rose

Rosa species and cultivars

'CHICAGO PEACE' is a sport of the famous 'Peace' rose but is hardier and has more vigorous growth. The colour is warm and rich.

CHEROKEE ROSE, Rosa laevigata, *is a beautiful wild rose with thorny stems. It is native to China and perhaps to America.*

FEATURES

THREE OF THE SHAPES common to rose bushes.

Throughout history the rose has been a symbol of life and love. It was known to the ancient Egyptians, the Greeks and the Romans, who grew roses in vast numbers. The Greek poet Sappho in 600 BC called it 'the queen of flowers'. Over the centuries the rose has gained many other symbolic meanings and it has had many uses. It is still used in the preparation of a range of cosmetics, food and medicine.

Wild roses grow around the Mediterranean, throughout the Middle East, Europe, North America and Asia, with the greatest number found in China. The apothecary's rose (*R. gallica* 'Officinalis') was introduced into Europe from its native Syria in the thirteenth century and roses were among the flowers depicted in the Dutch flower paintings of the early seventeenth century. In the late eighteenth century the introduction into Europe of the repeat flowering roses from China saw the beginning of rose hybridising on a large scale. Hybridising of roses has continued to this day.

Whole volumes have been devoted to roses and there is a vast literature available to anyone who wants to learn more about their history and the great range of roses that may be grown. There are, of course, the wild species, and then come Gallica, Damask, Alba, Moss, Centifolia, Portland, China, Tea, Noisette and Bourbon roses. In the nineteenth century the Hybrid Musk, Hybrid Perpetual and finally the Hybrid Tea roses were developed. It was from these that all the modern roses have come. Since the late 1960s there has been great interest in what are known as 'English' roses, which were bred by David Austin. These are recurrent flowering roses and they have the many-petalled form, lovely fragrance and full vigour of the much older roses.

Description Roses are loved for their form and colour and many are very fragrant. They can be evergreen or deciduous, and most varieties have prickled stems. In the right climate they can be very long lived, although they do not live as long in warmer climates. They reach maturity in 3–5 years and flower in 2 or 3 years. Some flower just once a year in spring while many others produce successive flushes of bloom. Flowers may be single, double or many petalled and there is a wide range of colours: white, cream, yellow, apricot, orange, every shade of pink and red, mauve and blue and bicoloured. Roses may be less than 25 cm in height or grow to 2 or 3 m or more. There are miniatures, shrubs, groundcovers (with miniature or normal-sized flowers), climbers and ramblers.

Uses Roses are lovely mass planted or as specimens—they may be grown as formal standard bushes or trained to weep to the ground from stems 2 m or more high—or simply as part of a mixed shrub border. Miniatures and polyantha roses are sometimes grown in containers, while hardy species such as *R. rugosa* are often used as hedges.

Whole gardens have been devoted to roses and they are always popular for planting in parks and municipal gardens. In large home gardens there may be special rose beds, while in the small garden a rose bush or two is often grown with other shrubs or surrounded by annuals, perennials or bulbs. Although some roses tolerate a degree of shade, the best situation is in full sun; many disease problems can be avoided if they are grown there.

CONDITIONS

Climate The hardiness of roses is variable. Many tolerate extreme cold while others are killed by frost. Wild roses are found from the Arctic to the tropics, thus the great variation.

'TOUR DE MALAKOFF', a Gallica-China hybrid raised in Britain in 1856. It can be more than 2 m high and may need support.

Aspect Roses need to have full sun all day to look their best. Good air circulation is important too but some shelter from very strong wind is desirable so that flowers are not damaged.

Soil Must have well-drained soil that has been prepared by adding large amounts of well-rotted manure or compost a few weeks before planting time. Add lime or dolomite to soils known to be very acid.

GROWING METHOD

Propagation Many roses strike fairly readily from cuttings of dormant wood taken in winter or very early spring. Others are more difficult and need to be budded onto understocks of species roses.

Watering Roses develop big root systems and so should be thoroughly soaked once or twice a week during the growing season.

Fertilising Use a complete plant food to fertilise roses in late winter or very early spring. Feed again after the first flowering flush and again in middle to late summer.

Problems Unfortunately roses may suffer from a number of disease problems and they can be attacked by a range of insects. Plant breeders are working hard to produce roses that have some resistance to these diseases. Some species and older roses do not succumb to these problems so readily.

*Rose scale covers the stems with a flaky looking small white scale. Small infestations can be controlled by scrubbing off with a soft brush. Badly infested stems should be pruned off or sprayed with white oil in the dormant season or with white oil and maldison in the growing period.

*Leaf cutting bees cut neat circular holes from the leaves but chemical control of these pests is not usually warranted.

*Fuller's rose weevil may chew ragged holes in leaves but unless damage is very severe you should not need to spray.

*Aphids, which are sap suckers, may cover new growth quite thickly. Wash off with a strong jet from the hose, wipe off or spray with soapy water or pyrethrum. This may need to be done every couple of days when aphids are numerous in spring and autumn.

*Nectar scarabs are small dark beetles that are often found in flowers. They feed on nectar and pollen and most of the damage is caused by the spines on their legs tearing the petals. Chemical control is rarely needed.

*Black spot is a fungal disease that produces black spots on leaves. Leaves may yellow and fall prematurely. This is a real problem in humid areas. Collect and destroy fallen leaves. Avoid overhead watering and water early in the day. Spraying with a fungicide such as triforine may be necessary. Some varieties are more prone to this disease than others.

*Powdery mildew is another fungal disease that produces grey-white patches on leaves and flower buds. Leaves and flowers that do open may be distorted. This occurs in warm to hot, humid weather. You should spray with wettable sulphur if the temperature is not too high or use a fungicide such as triforine. Some varieties are more susceptible than others.

*Rust and anthracnose are two other fungal problems in areas where humidity is high. Avoid overhead watering and water early in the day. Treatment with a fungicide registered for use with these diseases may be necessary.

FLOWERING

Season Depends on variety chosen. Some roses flower once only in spring but the display is often spectacular. Repeat flowering varieties have successive flushes of bloom from spring through until autumn. Some varieties produce brilliant red hips after flowering in autumn and are planted for this quality alone.

PRUNING

General Timing and severity of pruning depends on the type of rose. Those that flower once only are pruned after the spring blooming. Repeat flowering types are pruned in winter in milder areas or in early spring in very cold areas. Prune to an outward pointing leaf bud to keep the centre of the bush open.

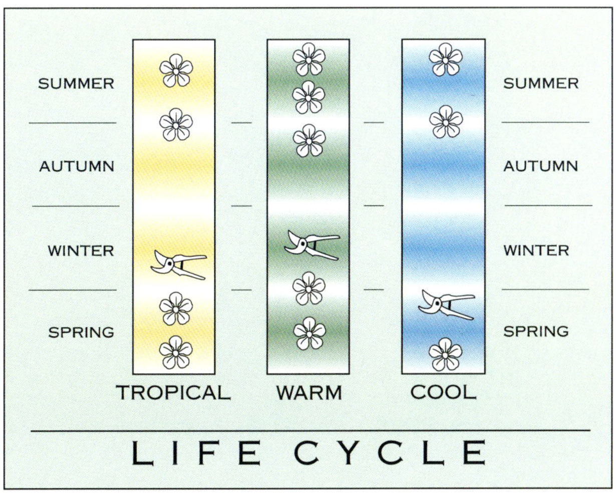

ROSE

LEFT: *'Double Delight' is indeed a double delight, having lovely two-toned flowers and a delicious fragrance. Introduced in the United States in 1977, it is very popular and unlikely to go out of fashion.*

RIGHT: *'Heidesommer' is a low, spreading rose that can be used as a groundcover. The foliage is a dark, glossy green and the small white flowers are lightly scented. It has a long flowering season.*

BELOW: *'Marina Prior' is a brilliant, clear red rose. Its long stems make it a favourite with many florists and flower arrangers.*

RIGHT: *'Golden Gloves' is a clear, golden yellow rose, shown here at the perfect midway stage between bud and full bloom. It is a vigorous grower, with very few thorns, and it is almost always in bloom.*

VARIETIES

LEFT: *'Claret Cup' is an Australian-bred polyantha rose, deep crimson with a white eye. Polyantha roses have a dwarf growth habit but bear large clusters of small flowers. They seem to have gone out of fashion—a pity as they give a great garden display.*

ABOVE: *'Bernina' is a cluster-flowered rose of compact growth. The rich, creamy yellow flowers are scented and perfectly formed. This rose was developed for, and named after, the Swiss sewing machine company.*

ABOVE: *'Purple Tiger', with its very unusual colour and striping, makes quite a conversation piece. Some people love it, but it doesn't suit everyone's taste.*

BELOW: *'Perfect Moment' is a lovely bicoloured rose in deep, creamy yellow with a rich crimson edging. It has a very shapely, high, pointed bud.*

Rosemary

Rosmarinus officinalis

AN AROMATIC SHRUB, rosemary has many uses but it's as pleasing in the garden as it is useful in the kitchen.

ROSEMARY FOR REMEMBRANCE: the distinctive scent of rosemary will stay with anyone who walks past this shrub.

FEATURES

This evergreen shrub is grown mainly for its aromatic foliage. Plant it where the aroma can be enjoyed whenever you pass. It can also be grown in a pot. The shrub reaches 1.5–2 m high and produces blue flowers in spring. It is long lived except in areas with wet or very humid summers, matures in 3–5 years and flowers from early in its life. Rosemary is a culinary herb; it is known as the herb of remembrance, love and fidelity. Prostrate rosemary (*R. lavandulaceus*) is ideal as a groundcover or spill-over plant.

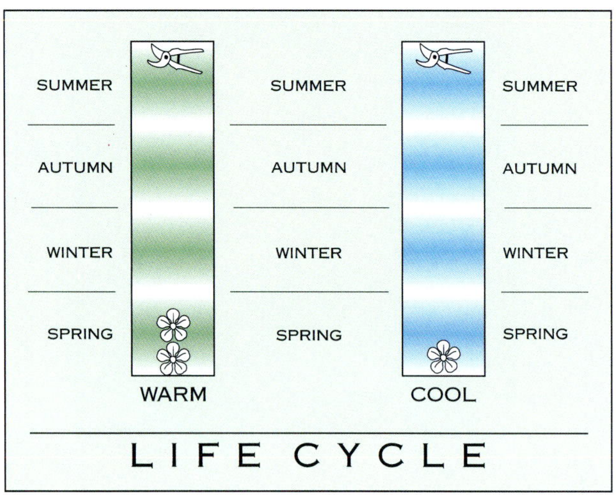

CONDITIONS

Climate Not suitable for the tropics but tolerates a wide range of climates. It does best in areas that have low humidity, hot summers and cool to cold winters.

Aspect Must have full sun all day for best results. It tolerates exposure to coastal winds.

Soil Must have very well-drained soil. Thrives in quite poor soil. Add lime or dolomite to soils known to be very acid.

GROWING METHOD

Propagation Grows readily from semi-hardwood cuttings taken during the months of late summer or early autumn.

Watering Needs regular watering to establish but once established tolerates quite long periods without water.

Fertilising Needs little or no fertiliser.

Problems No special insect pest or disease problems. Root rot will, however, kill plants if they are grown in heavy, poorly drained soils.

FLOWERING

Season The blue flowers are produced in spring.

PRUNING

General Trim after flowering to maintain dense, compact growth.

SACRED BAMBOO

Nandina domestica

BRIGHT RED BERRIES follow the small, white summer flowers of the Japanese sacred or heavenly bamboo, and the foliage is smart all year round.

UNLIKE TRUE BAMBOO, sacred bamboo is not invasive. It is ideal for a restricted space where height is required.

FEATURES

Sacred bamboo is a multi-stemmed evergreen shrub that slowly spreads with suckers to make a clump. The foliage is profuse but gives an impression of lightness. It is often used in Japanese-style gardens but can be used in any garden where foliage contrast with darker, heavier textured plants is needed. Small white flowers are followed by attractive red berries. In cool climates good autumn colour can be expected on the foliage. This long-lived shrub matures in 3–5 years, producing flowers and berries at that time. Reaching about 2 m high, sacred bamboo can be grown as an informal hedge or in mixed shrubberies. It can also be grown in a large container.

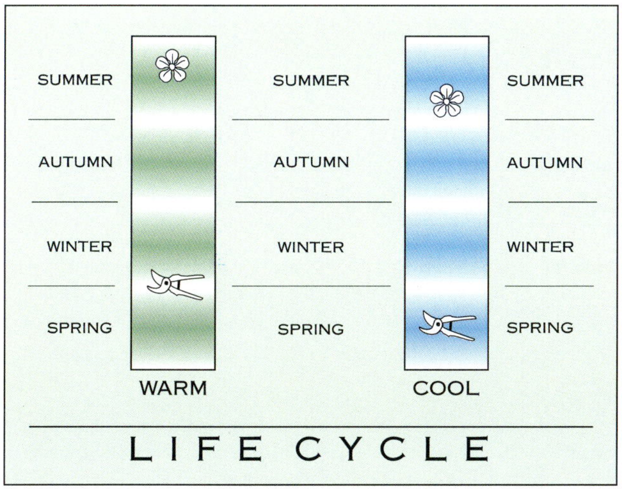

CONDITIONS

Climate Tolerates a wide range of climatic conditions and can be grown in quite cold zones. It is not suitable for tropical gardens.

Aspect Can be grown in full sun or semi-shade. Foliage colour varies according to site. In shade, leaves are pale green but in sun they take on reddish colours.

Soil Prefers well-drained soil that has been enriched with organic matter.

GROWING METHOD

Propagation Grow from seed sown in late winter or spring, or divide established clumps in late winter to early spring.

Watering Once established, this plant tolerates dry periods quite well but looks best if given deep regular watering in the warmer months.

Fertilising Apply blood and bone or complete plant food at the end of winter.

Problems No particular pest or disease problems.

FLOWERING

Season The small white flowers are produced in summer and early autumn.

Berries Attractive red berries follow the flowers and may persist through autumn and winter.

PRUNING

General Some of the oldest canes may be cut out at ground level in late winter or early spring to provide space for younger growths.

SPEEDWELL

***Hebe* species and cultivars**

HEBE ELLIPTICA *normally grows waist-high but it can be much larger. The flowers can be bright blue or white.*

THE ROUNDED HABIT of hebe 'Great Orme' contrasts here with upright cypresses. The splash of red in the background is a flame tree.

FEATURES

This large group of hardy evergreen shrubs is useful for many situations, including coastal planting as they tolerate exposed positions with salty winds. If kept pruned they have a reasonable life span, taking 3–5 years to maturity but flowering earlier. They reach 1–2 m or so high depending on variety. Flower colours are generally blue, mauve, pink and burgundy, with some varieties ageing to white to give a bicoloured effect. There are a great number of species and cultivars, and so try to purchase them in flower. Speedwells can be grown in mixed shrub borders or as low informal hedges, and the smaller types make good container plants.

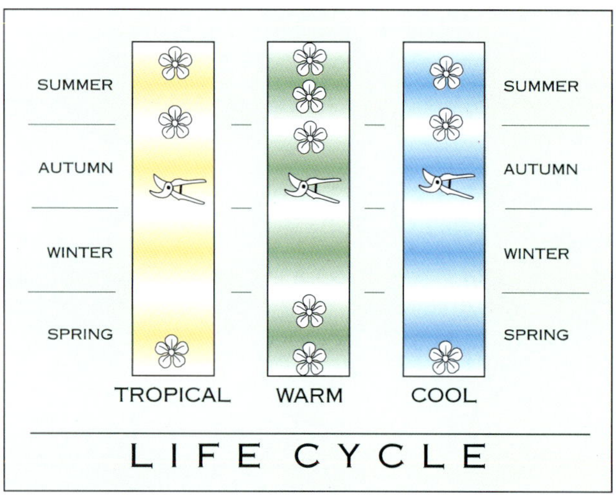

CONDITIONS

Climate Prefers a mild to warm climate but tolerates mild frosts. Some but not all are suitable for tropical gardens.

Aspect Needs an open position in full sun to grow to greatest potential.

Soil Must have well-drained soil. Added organic matter should improve growth rates but soils should never be too water retentive.

GROWING METHOD

Propagation Easiest to propagate from semi-hardwood cuttings taken in late summer and early autumn but soft-tip cuttings taken in spring can also be used.

Watering Needs regular watering to establish but once established tolerates dry periods quite well.

Fertilising Fertilise lightly during early spring with complete plant food, blood and bone or pelletted poultry manure.

Problems No specific pest or disease problems but heavy soils that retain water induce root rot.

FLOWERING

Season Most species and cultivars flower from middle to late spring through summer, some into early autumn. Many types have very long flowering periods.

PRUNING

General Prune after flowering to remove spent blooms and maintain dense growth.

Spur Flower

Plectranthus saccatus

DAINTY VIOLET TO BLUE FLOWERS and aromatic foliage are features of the spur flower. It grows best in warm climates.

SPUR FLOWER looks effective as a small shrub in this garden, but it can also be used as a tall groundcover.

FEATURES

A spreading evergreen shrub that is very easy to grow, the spur flower has aromatic foliage when crushed and violet to blue flowers that are produced over a long period. Rarely more than 60–70 cm high but spreading to 1 m or more wide, it may be used as a low shrub or as a taller groundcover. Spur flowers can also be grown in a container. They mature in about 2–3 years and flower from early in their life. They are not long-lived shrubs and it is best to take cuttings and start fresh plants after about 5 years.

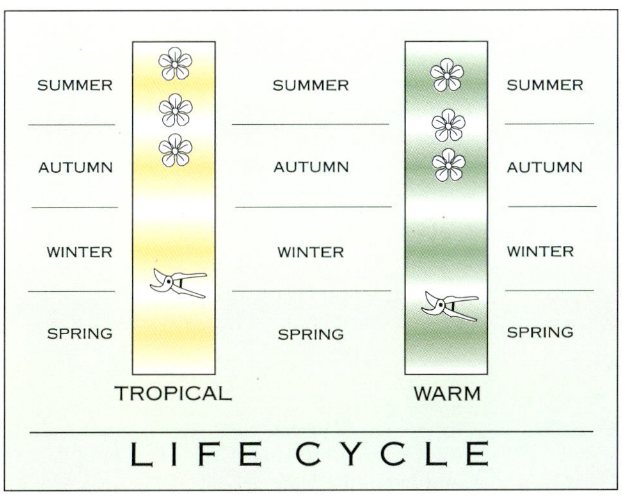

CONDITIONS

Climate Needs a warm, frost-free climate.

Aspect Needs shelter from strong wind. Dappled sunlight or morning sun and afternoon shade suit it best.

Soil Most average garden soils are suitable but they should be well drained.

GROWING METHOD

Propagation Grow from tip cuttings in spring and summer or from firmer wood in autumn and early winter. In the garden plants often layer themselves where they touch the ground.

Watering Needs regular watering to establish and deep soakings every week or two in warmer weather. Water regularly if the plant is in a sunny spot.

Fertilising Apply a light dressing of complete plant food in early spring.

Problems No particular pest or disease problems.

FLOWERING

Season Flowers are produced over a long period from midsummer to the middle of autumn.

Cutting Despite their fragile appearance, flowers cut well and are a great addition to posies.

PRUNING

General Remove spent blooms and cut back in late winter or early spring to maintain shape.

Star Magnolia

Magnolia stellata

FRAGRANT, STARRY WHITE FLOWERS cover the bare branches of the star magnolia, before the pale green leaves appear.

STAR MAGNOLIA as it looks best—growing on its own with nothing to distract from its glorious display of white flowers.

FEATURES

This deciduous, multi-stemmed shrub bears fragrant, white, star-like flowers. It is best displayed as a specimen or in a prominent spot in a mixed planting. There are some cultivars with pink flowers, of which the variety 'Water Lily' is probably the most outstanding. Most magnolias grow into quite large trees but this is ideal if you don't have room for a larger specimen as it grows to only 2–3 m high. Star magnolia is long lived, reaching maturity in 5–10 years and flowering after about 3 years.

CONDITIONS

Climate Prefers a warm climate and needs a sheltered site in cold zones.

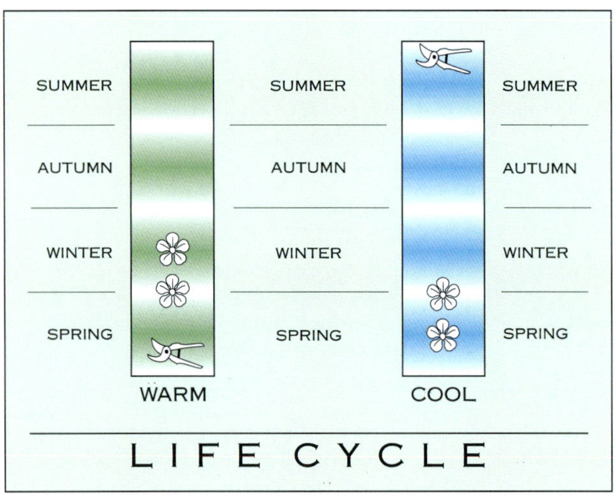

Aspect Needs shelter from strong wind and should be given sun for at least half a day to produce good flowering.

Soil Needs well-drained soil with plenty of organic matter incorporated well ahead of planting time. A good mulch of organic matter is beneficial too.

GROWING METHOD

Propagation Cuttings are difficult to root but can be attempted from semi-hardwood in late summer and autumn. Simple layering is most reliable and layers can be pegged down in late winter. They may take a year to root well.

Watering Needs regular deep watering, during spring and summer particularly.

Fertilising Apply blood and bone, or an azalea and camellia food, when leaf growth starts during early spring.

Problems The soft leaves can be browned or curled by hot, dry winds. Thrips may be a problem in a warm, dry spring too. Some birds find magnolia buds and flowers irresistible but this shrubby magnolia is not attacked as often as the tree-like *M.* x *soulangiana*.

FLOWERING

Season From middle to late winter in warm areas; spring in cool areas.

PRUNING

General May be tip pruned as flowers fade or at other times for shaping only. Heavier pruning is not necessary or desirable.

TEA-TREE

Leptospermum scoparium and cultivars

PINK IS MOST USUAL for the dainty flowers of the tea-tree but they also come in white and red. Branches cut when in bloom make excellent cut flowers.

TEA-TREE is an easy-to-grow, attractive shrub that thrives in all areas except the tropics.

FEATURES

These evergreen shrubs grow from 1 m or less to 3 m, depending on the variety. The flowers may be single or double, in pink, white or deep crimson, with pinks of every shade being predominant. Some cultivars show pink, white and red at the same time. Tea-trees may be short lived unless conditions are ideal and the shrub is kept pruned. They take 2–3 years to mature and flower from early in life. They may be displayed singly or mass planted.

CONDITIONS

Climate Not suitable for the tropics but tolerate a range of warm to cool climates and some frost. Suitable for coastal planting.

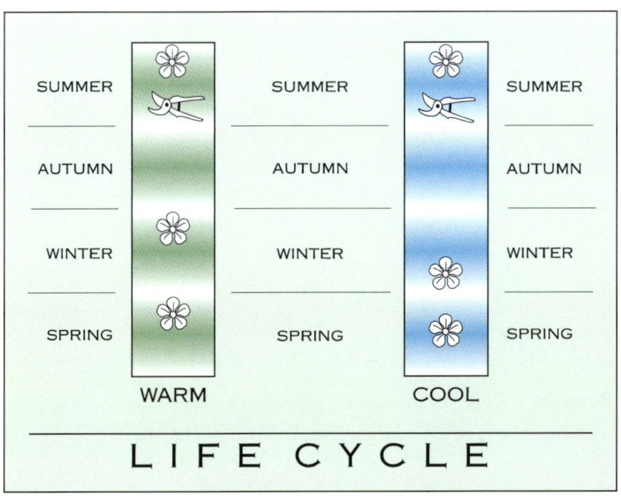

Aspect Needs full sun and good air circulation. Tolerates exposed windy sites well.

Soil Must have very well-drained soil. Mulching with very well-aged compost or leaf litter is an extra advantage.

GROWING METHOD

Propagation May be grown from soft-tip or semi-hardwood cuttings from spring through until autumn. Cuttings should be treated with hormone rooting gel or powder and then kept in a humid atmosphere.

Watering Needs regular water to establish. Then a deep watering every two weeks or so in hot, dry weather should be sufficient.

Fertilising Lightly feed with blood and bone or pelletted poultry manure.

Problems Plants are susceptible to root rot in heavy soils. Webbing caterpillars can be a nuisance and sprays are not very effective against these pests. Carefully check over your plant several times a year and cut or pull off damaged parts. The caterpillars are mostly in the webbed mass that is removed.

FLOWERING

Season Flowering time depends on variety chosen. Many flower in spring but some types flower from late autumn through winter to spring.

PRUNING

General Cut back after flowering but take care to cut only the lighter tip growth as cutting into old wood can be fatal.

THRYPTOMENE

Thryptomene saxicola

DAINTY PINK FLOWERS and small leaves combine to make thryptomene a popular and useful cut flower.

SLENDER, ARCHING STEMS of thryptomene are covered in small flowers for months from midwinter to the middle of spring. This is 'Pink Lace'.

FEATURES

An evergreen shrub, thryptomene has very small leaves and small flowers. The variety 'Payne's Hybrid' is most commonly grown and is valued for its long flowering period through winter and spring. The pale pink flowers, which are borne profusely on arching stems, last well in the vase and thryptomene is widely used by florists. In the garden, thryptomenes look most attractive when grown alone or in a mixed planting of shrubs. They grow from 1 to 1.5 m tall, taking 2–3 years to reach maturity but flowering from earlier in their life. Thryptomenes need to be replaced after 10 years at the most.

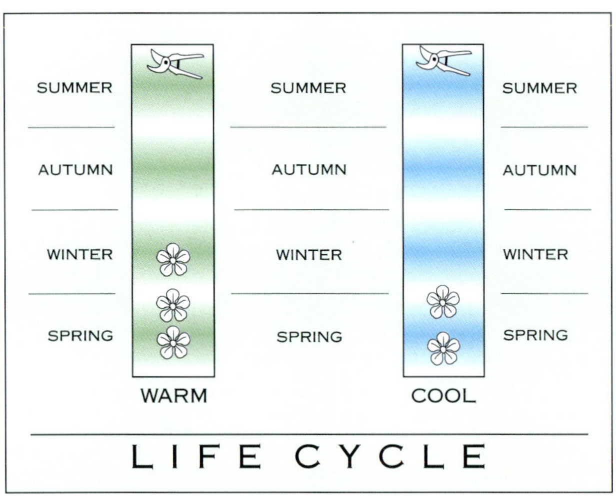

CONDITIONS

Climate Tolerates light frost but is best grown in areas with warm to hot summers and low humidity.

Aspect Needs full sun with shelter from very strong wind, although good air circulation is needed.

Soil Must have well-drained soil but the soil need not be very rich. Very heavy clay soils are not suitable for these shrubs unless plants can be grown on a mound.

GROWING METHOD

Propagation Semi-hardwood cuttings taken from late spring to early autumn should strike well. Using a hormone rooting powder increases the strike rate.

Watering Needs regular water to establish but once plants are established they tolerate long dry periods well.

Fertilising Feed lightly in early spring with blood and bone or slow release granular fertiliser.

Problems No particular insect pest or disease problems.

FLOWERING

Season Long flowering period from middle of winter through to middle of spring.

PRUNING

General Should be cut back after flowering has finished to maintain a dense growth habit. Cutting flowers for the vase during the flowering season is one way of pruning.

VIBURNUM

Viburnum species and cultivars

SOME VIBURNUMS lend themselves to use as hedges but the wide-spreading Viburnum plicatum *looks best shown off on its own.*

STAR OF THIS SPRING GARDEN is Viburnum x burkwoodii *with its abundant clusters of fragrant, tubular flowers of palest pink.*

FEATURES

The flowers of this large group of long lived, evergreen and deciduous shrubs are white, although some have a faint pink tinge. Most are sweetly perfumed. Viburnums grow from 1 to 3 m or more high and take 5–10 years to mature, most species flowering within 3 years. Some, such as the evergreen *V. tinus*, are often grown as screening plants or informal hedges while the deciduous *V. plicatum* makes a lovely specimen or feature. Many varieties are grown in mixed shrub borders as background plants.

CONDITIONS

Climate Best in mild to cool climates and not suitable for the tropics. In areas where late frosts may be a problem they should be grown in a sheltered position.

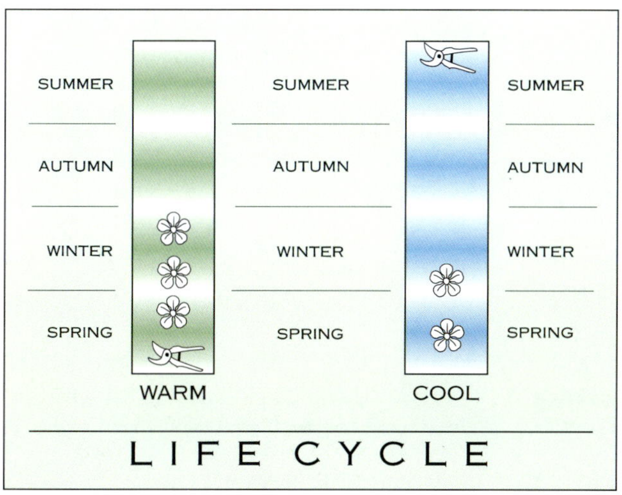

Aspect Needs at least half a day's sun and in cool climates full sun all day. Varieties that bear large flowers are best given some form of protection from wind.

Soil Prefers well-drained soil that has been enriched with decayed organic matter well before planting time. Mulching with organic matter is beneficial and helps to retain moisture and to keep roots cool during the summer months.

GROWING METHOD

Propagation Most viburnums can be grown from semi-hardwood cuttings taken during late summer or early autumn but deciduous species grow well from cuttings of dormant wood taken during winter. For varieties that are hard to strike, try layering.

Watering Give deep regular watering in dry weather during the warmer months.

Fertilising Feed with complete plant food or blood and bone as flowering finishes in spring.

Problems Most have few problems but *V. tinus* is often disfigured by mites or thrips in warm districts.

FLOWERING

Season Most viburnums are spring flowering, some commencing in late winter. *V. tinus*, however, flowers through winter into early spring.

PRUNING

General Trim lightly after flowering to remove spent blooms. Thinning out dense growth from the centre of the bush may be needed too. Multi-stemmed types may need to have some of the older canes cut out at ground level to make way for new growth.

WARATAH

Telopea speciosissima

ADMIRED THROUGHOUT THE WORLD, the waratah is traditionally red, but it can also be white or even pink.

THE STATELY WARATAH grows best in mild climates and is quite fussy about its needs. It will last up to two weeks in the vase.

FEATURES

An evergreen shrub that may grow to 3 m in good conditions, the waratah is a distinctive Australian shrub grown for its striking crimson flower. They are usually grown in mixed shrub plantings but would look spectacular mass planted. Cultivated varieties such as 'Shady Lady' seem to be easier to grow than the straight species. Waratahs have a moderate life span but can be long lived in ideal conditions if they are cut back regularly. They flower after about 3 years and reach maturity in 3–5 years.

CONDITIONS

Climate Best in mild climates with only light frosts. Other species, such as *T. oreades* and *T. mongaensis*, tolerate much cooler climates.

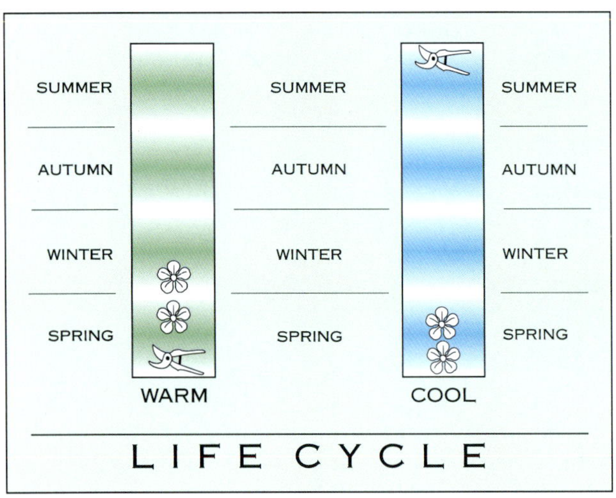

Aspect Suitable for either full sun or semi-shade.

Soil Must have very well-drained soil with no added nutrients. A thick mulch of bark, leaf litter or very well-decayed compost is most beneficial but mulch should be kept well clear of the stem.

GROWING METHOD

Propagation Can be grown from seed planted in late winter. Sow seeds in small individual pots to avoid disturbing roots when planting out. Selected varieties are grown from leaf bud cuttings but this is not easy for the home gardener.

Watering Needs regular watering to establish but once established it is best to restrict watering to occasional deep soakings. Watering is most important in autumn and in late winter and spring to coincide with growth spurts.

Fertilising Do not fertilise at all.

Problems Waratahs are very susceptible to root rot if the soil is heavy and moisture retentive. Watch out for signs of moth borer attack: sawdust or frass in the forks of the stems are characteristic signs. Remove the sawdust and webbing by hand or with a brush.

FLOWERING

Season Flowers appear in early spring and last for several weeks.

Cutting Waratah is an excellent cut flower.

PRUNING

General Flowers, fresh or spent, should be cut with long stems as a form of pruning. Young plants should be tip pruned regularly to produce more potentially flowering wood.

Wattle

Acacia

STRIKING YELLOW FLOWER SPIKES and silver-grey foliage are features of Acacia glaucescens *(syn.* A. binervia*), the coast myall.*

MOUNT MORGAN OR QUEENSLAND WATTLE has scented, bright yellow flowers. It is one of the fastest growing of all wattles.

FEATURES

There are around 900 species of wattle, and so there is one to suit every situation. Wattles are evergreen shrubs or trees that produce yellow or cream flowers in fluffy balls or rods. They come in a wide variety of leaf shapes and many are very sweetly scented. There are many shrubby wattles that grow 3–4 m high but the total range is from about 1–2 m up to 5–6 m. Some tree-like species grow to 10–20 m high. Most wattles are very fast growing and although some are short-lived they can be replaced quite quickly. Depending on species, they mature in about 3–5 years and flower from early in life. Wattles may be used as screening plants, windbreaks, garden specimens or in mixed plantings. As many species bloom in winter, they are a valuable addition to the garden. Flower buds can be seen forming on the plant many months before the actual blooming period.

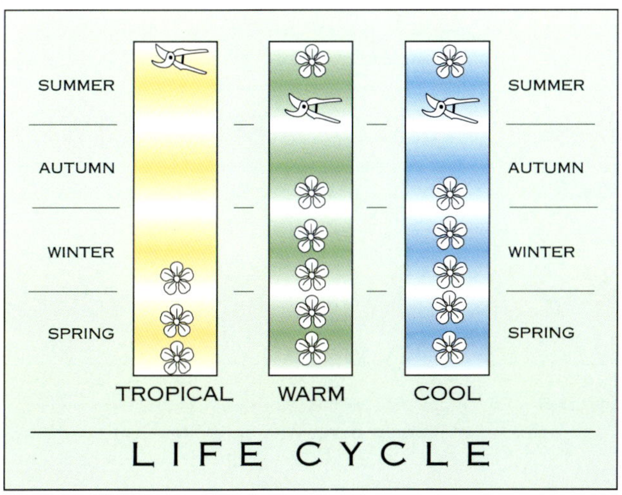

CONDITIONS

Climate There is a wattle species to suit most climates, from cool, high rainfall areas to arid regions and the tropics. Most nurseries stock species suitable for their district.

Aspect Most need full sun all day but some species tolerate semi-shade or dappled sunlight.

Soil Most prefer well-drained soils but some species grow well in heavier clays.

GROWING METHOD

Propagation Easy to grow from seed that needs soaking overnight to soften the hard seed coat. Immerse seed in very hot water and leave overnight or for several hours; sow at once.

Watering Needs regular watering to establish but once established tolerates long periods of dry weather. Occasional deep watering keeps shrubs in good condition.

Fertilising Fertilising is not essential; plants may be fed lightly with blood and bone in early spring.

Problems Moth borers frequently attack wattles and so plants should be inspected regularly and sawdust and webbing removed. Water more regularly if this is a problem. There are a number of sap-sucking insects that may attack wattles but control is difficult. Improving the vigour of the shrub is usually the best defence.

FLOWERING

Season There is a wattle in bloom every month of the year but a great many flower through winter and spring.

PRUNING

General Not essential but shrubs can be trimmed after flowering to improve their shape.

WEDDING BELLS

Deutzia

IN THIS CORNER of a spring garden, white wedding bells make a charming background to a border of yellow English primrose.

WEDDING BELLS is a deciduous shrub from China and Japan. Its small but abundant bell-shaped flowers can be white or pale pink.

FEATURES

These multi-stemmed deciduous shrubs are easy to grow and are usually seen in mixed shrubberies or as background plants to displays of spring flowering annuals and bulbs. There are many species and cultivars: they range in height from 1 to 3 m. Long lived, especially if old canes are cut out regularly, wedding bells flower from early in their life and mature in about 5 years. Wedding bells mostly have white flowers, which can be single or double, but there are also some pink flowered cultivars available.

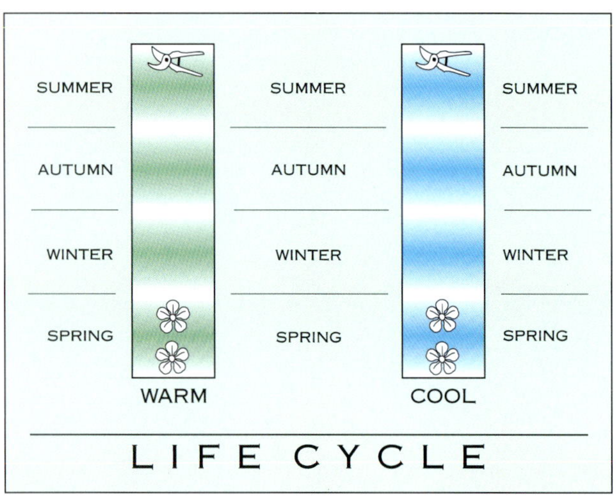

CONDITIONS

Climate Best in cool, moist districts but they tolerate warm zones. Not suitable for the tropics.

Aspect Need full sun and protection from very strong wind. In warmer areas plants prefer morning sun and afternoon shade.

Soil Must have well-drained soil enriched with organic matter before planting. Mulching with well-decayed compost or manure is beneficial.

GROWING METHOD

Propagation Easiest from hardwood cuttings of dormant wood taken during winter but may also be grown from semi-hardwood cuttings taken in late summer and early autumn.

Watering Need regular deep watering throughout the spring and summer months.

Fertilising Apply complete plant food or blood and bone in early spring.

Problems No specific insect pest or disease problems.

FLOWERING

Season All varieties flower in spring.

PRUNING

General Trim off spent flower heads immediately after blooming. Remove some of the older canes at ground level at the same time to make way for new, vigorous growth.

Weigela

Weigela florida and cultivars

TRUMPET SHAPED, the flowers of Weigela florida *open pale pink and become deeper pink.*

A VARIEGATED DWARF WEIGELA with white flowers here makes a graceful background plant, intermingled with a pink-flowering comfrey.

FEATURES

A deciduous, multi-stemmed shrub usually growing 2–3 m high, weigela has flowers mostly in shades of pink, with some white and deep crimson flowered cultivars. Some cultivars have variegated cream and green foliage. Weigela is long lived, especially if old canes are cut out regularly. It matures in about 5 years and flowers from early in life. This fast-growing shrub makes a graceful background plant or screen, even when leafless in winter.

CONDITIONS

Climate Grows in warm to quite cold zones; not suitable for arid areas or the tropics.

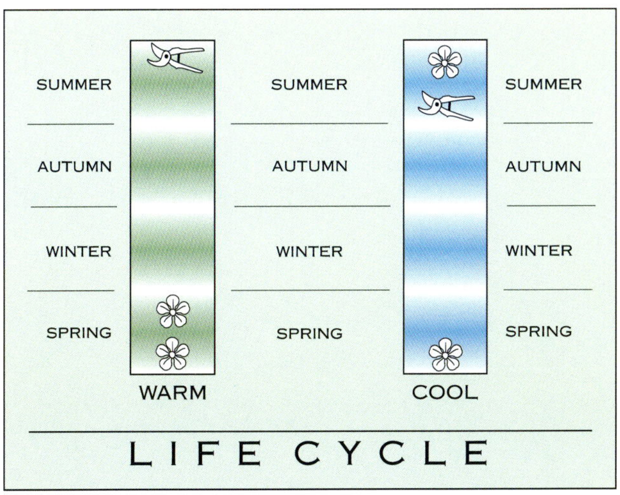

Aspect Needs full sun and prefers shelter from strong wind. Strong wind damages flowers and may also burn the margins of soft new leaves, causing them to go brown.

Soil Needs well-drained soil enriched with large amounts of well-decayed manure or compost before planting. Mulching with organic matter improves growth too.

GROWING METHOD

Propagation Easiest from hardwood cuttings of dormant wood taken in winter but plants can also be propagated from tip cuttings of new growth in late spring.

Watering Needs regular deep watering throughout spring and summer.

Fertilising Apply complete plant food in early spring. Pelletted poultry manure or blood and bone are also suitable.

Problems No specific insect pest or disease problems.

FLOWERING

Season Flowers profusely throughout spring; later in cool areas.

Cutting Stems may be cut for indoor decoration.

PRUNING

General Some of the oldest canes should be cut out at ground level after flowering to make way for the new growth. This also rejuvenates the shrub. It is best not to prune the flowered shoots as this tends to spoil the natural growth habit of the plant.

FLOWERING CHART

PLANT COMMON NAME	SUITABLE CLIMATE	SPRING EARLY	SPRING MID	SPRING LATE	SUMMER EARLY	SUMMER MID	SUMMER LATE	AUTUMN EARLY	AUTUMN MID	AUTUMN LATE	WINTER EARLY	WINTER MID	WINTER LATE
Abelia	🟡🟢🔵				🟡🟢🔵	🟡🟢🔵	🟢🔵						
Ardisia	🟡🟢🔵	🟡	🟢		🔵								
Azalea	🟢🔵	🟢		🔵									🟢
Banksia	🟡🟢🔵	🔵								🟡🟢🔵	🟡🟢🔵	🟡🟢🔵	🟡🟢🔵
Barberry	🟢🔵	🟢🔵											
Bauhinia	🟡🟢					🟡🟢	🟡🟢	🟡🟢					
Begonia	🟡🟢		🟡🟢	🟡🟢	🟡🟢	🟡🟢	🟡🟢	🟡	🟡				
Bird of paradise	🟡🟢	🟡🟢	🟡							🟡🟢	🟡🟢	🟡🟢	🟡🟢
Blue butterfly bush	🟡🟢			🟡	🟡🟢	🟡🟢	🟡🟢	🟡					
Boronia	🟢🔵	🟢🔵	🔵	🔵								🟢	🟢
Bottlebush	🟡🟢🔵	🟡	🟢🔵	🟢🔵			🟡	🟢🔵					
Box	🟢🔵	🟢	🔵										
Butterfly bush	🟢🔵				🟢🔵	🟢🔵	🟢🔵	🟢🔵					
Californian lilac	🟢🔵	🟢🔵	🟢🔵	🟢🔵	🔵	🔵							
Camellia	🟢🔵	🟢🔵						🟢	🟢	🟢🔵	🟢🔵	🟢🔵	🟢🔵
Cassia	🟡🟢🔵	🟢🔵	🟢🔵	🟢🔵	🔵	🟡	🟡	🟡🟢					
Cherry pie	🟡🟢			🟡🟢	🟡🟢	🟡🟢	🟡🟢						
Chinese lantern	🟡🟢🔵	🟡🟢	🟡🟢	🟡🟢	🟡🟢🔵								
Coast rosemary	🟡🟢🔵	🟡🟢	🟡🟢	🟢🔵	🟢🔵								
Coral plant	🟡🟢	🟡🟢	🟡🟢	🟡🟢	🟡🟢	🟡🟢	🟡🟢	🟡🟢					
Cotoneaster	🟢🔵		🟢🔵	🟢🔵									
Croton													
Crowea	🟡🟢	🟡🟢	🟡🟢	🟡🟢						🟡🟢	🟡🟢	🟡🟢	🟡🟢
Daphne	🟢🔵	🔵	🔵									🟢	🟢
Diosma	🟡🟢	🟢	🟢									🟡	🟡🟢
Dog rose	🟢🔵	🟢	🟢	🟢🔵									
Eriostemon	🟢	🟢	🟢										🟢
Escallonia	🟢🔵		🟢	🟢🔵	🟢🔵	🔵	🔵						
Euphorbia	🟢🔵	🟢	🟢	🟢🔵	🔵								🟢
Euryops	🟡🟢🔵	🟡🟢🔵	🟡🟢🔵	🟡🟢🔵							🟡🟢	🟡🟢	🟡🟢
Fijian fire plant	🟡🟢				🟡🟢	🟡🟢	🟡🟢	🟡🟢					
Firethorn	🟢🔵			🟢🔵									
Gardenia	🟡🟢			🟡🟢	🟡🟢	🟡🟢	🟡🟢						
Geraldton wax	🟢🔵	🟢🔵	🟢🔵	🟢🔵								🟢	🟢🔵
Grevillea	🟡🟢🔵	🟡🟢🔵	🟡🟢🔵	🟡🟢🔵	🟡🟢🔵								🟡🟢
Hakea	🟡🟢🔵	🟡🟢🔵	🟢🔵	🟢🔵				🟢	🟢	🟢	🟢	🟢	🟡🟢🔵
Hawthorn	🟢🔵		🟢🔵										
Heath	🟢🔵	🟢🔵	🟢🔵							🔵	🔵	🔵	🟢🔵
Hibiscus (*H. rosa-sinensis*)	🟡🟢			🟡	🟡🟢	🟡🟢	🟡🟢	🟡🟢	🟡🟢	🟡🟢			
Hibiscus (*H. syriacus*)	🟢🔵				🟢🔵	🟢🔵	🟢🔵	🟢🔵					
Honey-myrtle	🟡🟢🔵	🟡🟢	🟡🟢	🟡🟢🔵	🟡🟢🔵								🟢
Honeysuckle	🟢🔵			🟢	🟢🔵	🟢🔵	🟢🔵					🟢	🟢🔵
Hydrangea	🟡🟢🔵			🟡🟢	🟡🟢🔵	🟢🔵	🟢🔵	🔵					
Indian hawthorn	🟢🔵	🟢🔵	🔵	🔵									🟢

CLIMATE KEY: ○ TROPICAL (T) ● WARM (W) ● COOL (C)

PLANT COMMON NAME	SUITABLE CLIMATE	SPRING EARLY	SPRING MID	SPRING LATE	SUMMER EARLY	SUMMER MID	SUMMER LATE	AUTUMN EARLY	AUTUMN MID	AUTUMN LATE	WINTER EARLY	WINTER MID	WINTER LATE
Indigo plant	W C		W	W	W C	W C	W C						
Ixora	T W				T	T W	T W	T	T				
Japonica	W C	C										W	W C
Justicia	T W				T W	T W	T W	T W	T W				
Kerria	W C	W	W	W C									
Lantana	T W		T W	T W	T W	T	T						
Lasiandra	T W						T W	T W	T W	T W	T		
Lavender	W C	W	W	W C	W C								W
Lilac	C	C	C	C	C								
Luculia	T W								T W	T W	T W	T W	
Mahonia	W C	W C	W C	W C								W	W
May	W C	W	W	W C									
Mexican orange blossom	T W C	T W	T W	T W C									
Mint bush	W C	W	W	W C	C								
Misty plume bush	T W										T W	T W	
Morning, noon & night	T W	T W	T W	T W									
Oleander	T W C			T	T W	T W	T W C	W	W				
Orange browallia	T W	T W	T W	T W	T								T W
Orange jessamine	T W			T W	T W								
Pentas	T W			T W	T W	T W	T W	T W	T W	T W			
Photinia	W C		W	C									
Pieris	W C	W C	W C										W
Plumbago	T W			T	T W	T W	T W	T W					
Poinsettia	T W								T	T W	T W	T W	T
Pomegranate	W C			W C	W C	W C	W C						
Port wine magnolia	T W	T W	T W	T W									
Pride of Madeira	T W C	T W	T W	T W C	C								
Prunus	W C	W C											W
Rhododendron	W C	C	W C	W C			W C	W C	W C	W C	W		
Rock rose	W C			W C	C	C	C						
Rondeletia	T W	T W	T W	W									T
Rose	T W C	T W	T W	T W C	T W C	T W C	T W C	T W C					W
Rosemary	W C	W	W	W C									
Sacred bamboo	W C				W	W C	C	C					
Speedwell	T W C	W	W	T W C	T W C	T W C	T W C	W					
Spur flower	T W				T	T W	T W	T W	T W				
Star magnolia	W C	C	C									W	W
Tea-tree	W C	W	C		W C							W	C
Thryptomene	W C	W C	W C	W C	W							W	W
Viburnum	W C	W C	C								W	W	W C
Waratah	W C	W	W C	C									W
Wattle	T W C	T W C	T W C	T W	W C					W C	W C	W C	T W C
Wedding bells	W C	W C	W C	W C									
Weigela	W C	W	W	W C	C								

INDEX

Page numbers in *italics* refer to illustrations

Published by Murdoch Books®, a division of Murdoch Magazines Pty Ltd,
213 Miller Street, North Sydney NSW 2060

Designer: Annette Fitzgerald
Series and Cover Design: Jackie Richards
Editor: Christine Eslick
Photographs: Lorna Rose (all unless specified otherwise); Stirling Macoboy (pp. 21R, 25R, 64L, 106R)
Illustrator: Matthew Ottley

Publisher: Anne Wilson
Publishing Manager: Catie Ziller
Managing Editor: Susan Tomnay
Studio Manager: Norman Baptista
Production Co-ordinator: Liz Fitzgerald
International Manager: Mark Newman
Marketing Manager: Mark Smith
National Sales Manager: Keith Watson
Key Accounts Sales Manager: Kim Deacon
Photo Librarian: Dianne Bedford

National Library of Australia
Cataloguing-in-Publication Data
Hanks, Margaret
A grower's guide to flowering shrubs
Includes index
ISBN 0 86411 423 0
1. Flowering shrubs. I. Title
635.976

Printed by Prestige Litho, Queensland

Acknowledgements
The publisher would like to thank the following for allowing photography: Mrs Dell Adam, Sydney NSW (pp. 32L, 33R, 87R, 91L, 100R); Ashcombe Maze, Shoreham Vic. (pp. 43R, 72R); Belrose Nursery, Belrose NSW (pp. 40L, 50L, 101R); Burnbank, Ladysmith NSW (p. 36R); Buskers End, Bowral NSW (p. 107L); Camellia Grove Nursery, St Ives NSW (pp. 12R, 14 top L and bottom L); Cataract Gorge, Launceston Tas. (pp. 13, 14 bottom R); Centennial Park, Sydney (p. 57R); Curry Flat, Nimmitabel NSW (pp. 36L, 53L, 103L); Dunedin, St Leonards Tas. (pp. 44R, 68L); Janet Dunlop, Orange NSW (pp. 39L, 53R); Eryldene, Gordon NSW (pp. 12C and bottom R, 27L, 30L); Fairyburn, Orange NSW (p. 70L); Mrs Ailsa Ferguson, Killara NSW (p. 41L and R); Foxglove Spires, Tilba Tilba NSW (pp. 9, 64B, 107R); Mrs Bette Hardwicke, Pymble NSW (p. 38R); Heronswood, Dromana Vic. (pp. 4, 32R, 86L and R); Mrs Eileen Hogbin, Mt Kuring-gai NSW (p. 103R); Kennerton Green, Mittagong NSW (p. 8); Kiah Park, Jaspers Brush NSW (pp. 50R, 72L, 106L); Kooringal, Wagga Wagga NSW (p. 67L and R); Lindfield Park, Mt Irvine NSW (p. 98R); Kate and Peter MacNeil, Wagga Wagga NSW (p. 90L); Betty Maloney, Frenchs Forest NSW (p. 42R); Morella, Bruny Island Tas. (pp. 15 top L, 22L, 52R, 89 top L); Mt Tomah Botanic Gardens, NSW (p. 98L); Parkers Nursery, Turramurra NSW (pp. 24R, 102R); Mrs Annette Payne, Beecroft NSW (p. 82R); Quincey Cottage, Blue Mountains NSW (pp. 25L, 33L); Rose Cottage, Beechworth Vic. (p. 85L and R); Royal Botanic Gardens, Sydney (pp. 58L and R, 60R, 61L and R, 63R, 79L and R, 96L, 104L); Mary Rutledge, Longford Tas. (p. 26L); Dora Scott, Wahroonga NSW (pp. 19R, 27R, 35R, 63L); Shirley, Holts Flat NSW (pp. 43L, 96R); Mrs Pat Taylor, St Ives NSW (pp. 44L, 62L and R); Ann Thomson Garden Advisory Service, St Ives NSW (pp. 30R, 39R, 87L); Tour de Malakoff Rose Nursery, Beechworth Vic. (p. 68R); Tregamere, Te Awamutu NZ (pp. 12L, 101L); Vireya Vale, Mt Pleasant NSW (pp. 89 bottom L and R, 100L); Weerona, Wagga Wagga NSW (pp. 23R, 45R); Woodleigh Farm Garden, Marton NZ (pp. 24L, 92L); Yengo, Mt Wilson NSW (p. 70R)

Front cover: Lasiandra (*Tibouchina*) flowers
Back cover: Top left: Waratah (*Telopea* 'Shady Lady'; top centre: pride of Madiera (*Echium fastuosum*); top right: *Photinia fraseri* 'Robusta'. Bottom left: *Grevillea juniperina* 'Pink Lady'; bottom centre: tea-tree (*Leptospermum scoparium* 'Nanum Rubrum'; bottom right: *Euphorbia*
Inside front cover: A colourful collection of mixed roses
Title page: 'Buttons 'n' Bows', a formal double hybrid of *Camellia saluenensis*